The Bingo Report

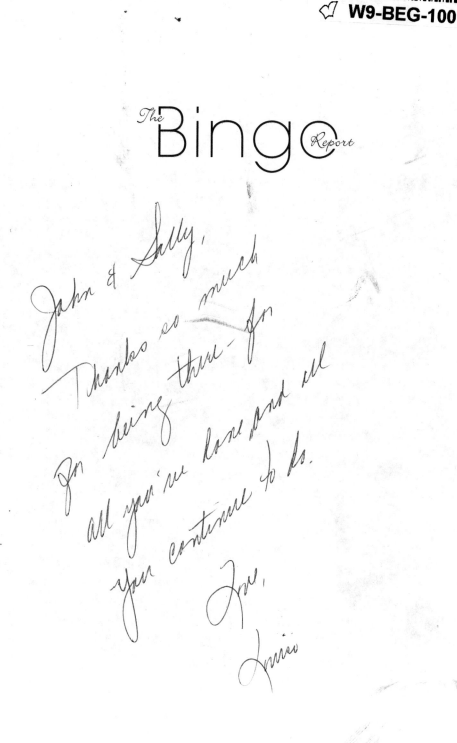

John & Sally,

Thanks so much
for being there—for
all you've done and all
you continue to do.

Love,

Louise

For information about permission to reproduce
sections from this book, write to:

Center for the Study of Religious Issues
P.O. Box 246
Freeport, ME 04032

CSRI99@aol.com

For additional copies, send $17.95 (U.S.)
plus $3.95 postage and handling to:

   CSRI Books
   P. O. Box 246
   Freeport, ME 04032

ISBN: 0-9770402-0-8
Library of Congress: applied for

A portion of this book was presented at the 1999 and 2000
annual conferences of the Society of Scientific Study of Religion
and Eastern Sociological Society.

Printed in the United States of America.

Cover and Interior Design: Cheryl Carrington

The Bingo Report

Mandatory Celibacy and Clergy Sexual Abuse

LOUISE HAGGETT

Center for the Study of Religious Issues

Freeport, Maine

FOR JESUS,

MY MOM, YVONNE BLANCHE GOUSSE,

MY GUARDIAN ANGEL AND INSPIRATION,

AND MY DAD RAOUL OVIDE LABBÉ,

WHO TAUGHT ME TO STAND UP FOR TRUTH AND JUSTICE.

THIS BOOK IS ALSO DEDICATED TO

THE HANDFUL OF PRIESTS WHO JEOPARDIZED THEIR

CAREERS BY TESTIFYING FOR THE VICTIMS

IN CLERGY SEXUAL ABUSE COURT CASES;

ALSO FOR THE VICTIMS/SURVIVORS

WHO CAME FORWARD WITH THEIR STORIES,

PARTICULARLY THOSE WHO ASSISTED IN OUR RESEARCH.

Contents

List of Tables

Chapter Two—Priest Study

Preface

The title "Bingo" came to me in a dream several years ago. Observations I had made and cursory research I had done regarding the Roman Catholic priesthood made me wonder if it was connected to clergy sexual abuse. In my dream, I envisioned a Bingo card with the words "mandatory celibacy" and "clergy sexual abuse" intertwined with one another like a crossword puzzle. One of the sociologists who read the manuscript agreed that the name was very fitting because it sounded very "Catholic."

In the fall of 2004, my husband and I attended a local dinner and seminar. Sitting across from us was a German physicist and his wife, who turned out to be members of one of the eighty-three Catholic churches scheduled to close in the Boston diocese. At one point during the evening, the conversation turned to my research and this book. The physicist asked what I planned to title my book. When I replied, "Bingo," his eyes lit up and he exclaimed, "You mean 'Eureka!'"

And so, the name has stuck.

Acknowledgments

First and foremost, I thank Professor Lucille Lawless at Framingham State College, who introduced me to the field of sociology in 1994, and who was interested enough in my curiosities about the Catholic Church that she spent tireless hours over a ten-year period mentoring me throughout this project. Without her assistance, this research and book would never have been possible.

Thanks to Rev. Walter Wrobel for initiating my curiosity by unsolicitingly, for a number of years, sending me a myriad of scientific journal articles on child sexual abuse and on mandatory celibacy in the Roman Catholic priesthood. Thanks also to Framingham State College librarian Neil Conrad for helping me obtain countless other research documents.

Thanks to the readers and editors of this report: Dick Haggett, Lucille Lawless, Jim Schooley, Frank McGrath, Dick Lesser, Jansen String, Margie Slater, Kay Goodnow, Lonnie Corey, Frances Salone-Pelletier, Jean Pelletier, Lee Ganim, Rosann Ganim, Kathleen Kautzer, Frances Minderlein, Ed Minderlein, F. Peter Szafran, Judge Elbert Tuttle, Steve Sabanos and Bob Land.

I must also acknowledge those who encouraged the work, especially at times when I became overwhelmed and discouraged. The support system was tremendous and included my beloved husband Dick; our son Greg and his family; my siblings Pauline Thompson, Dick Labbe, Lonnie Corey Byers, and Conni String; my devoted friends Jean Vacca, Margie Slater, (the late) Norman and Barbara Savoy, Anita Damiano and William and Donna Podobinski; the CITI Ministries Board of Directors and Advisory Committee: Jim Schooley, Fr. John Shuster, Joe Maher, Fr. Rich Hasselbach, Fr. Steve Sabanos, Fr. Lee and Rosann Ganim, Fr. Bob and Jean Scanlan, Sally Dowling, Fr. Pete Szafran, (the late) Fr. Jim and Mary Jane Harris, Fr. Frank McGrath, Fr. Joe McOscar, Fr. Jim Magmer, and Fr. Jean and Frances Salone-Pelletier; and CITI's office staff, Jeremy Mulligan, Eleanor Randall, Ginny Stafford and Andy Otto.

Special thanks also to Fr. A. W. Richard Sipe, Fr. Tom Doyle, Dr. Dean Hoge, Rev. Dr. Heinz-Jurgen Vogels, the late Paolo Camellini, the late Fr. Tom Economus, Frances Kissling, Tom Kerwin, and Charlie Davis for their support.

LH

I would like to acknowledge at the outset that, according to psychotherapist and celibacy researcher A. W. Richard Sipe, only 2 percent of the Roman Catholic clergy receive as part of their calling to the priesthood the true charism or gift of celibacy/chastity. *The Bingo Report* might then be about those priests for whom mandatory celibacy is a struggle.

"Then you will know the truth
. . . and the truth will set you free."

John 8:32

Glossary

Bishop—A bishop carries on the work of the apostles. By reason of Episcopal consecration, he shares in the triple apostolic function of teacher of doctrine, priest of sacred worship, and minister of church government. Bishops are responsible for the pastoral care of their dioceses. In addition, bishops have a responsibility to act in council to guide the church. The United States is divided into provinces consisting of several dioceses. This division is usually by state with the major diocese (in Massachusetts=Boston) being considered an Archdiocese and the bishop being the Archbishop. While the Archbishop usually has great influence over who is appointed bishop in the other dioceses in his province, once appointed, the local bishop is in full control of his own diocese.

Canon Lawyer—Lawyer, usually a priest, who specializes in the Code of Canon Law, the official body of laws for the Catholic Church.

Cardinal—Cardinals are chosen by the Pope to assist in the worldwide management of the church. Outside of Rome, bishops of major dioceses may be named Cardinals, such as in some of the major dioceses in the United States: New York, Chicago, Los Angeles and Washington D.C. While a Cardinal may have more influence because of his title, he exercises no special authority over local bishops.

Celibacy—The practice of perfect continence by priests and bishops meant to foster single-minded devotion to God and service in the ministry. According to the long-standing discipline of the Latin Rite Church (since 1139), the rule of celibacy forbids marriage by priests and bishops, and it normally excludes married persons from ordination.

Chastity—The virtue which tempers, regulates and moderates our sexual desires, thoughts and actions. Religious order priests only, take the vow of chastity.

Child Sexual Abuse—According to Sociologist David Finkelhor (1994), legal and research definitions require two elements:

1) sexual activities involving a child and 2) an "abusive condition."

1. Sexual activities involving a child
   a. Contact sexual abuse—involves touching sexual portions of partner's body, whether or not there is penetration
   b. Non-contact sexual abuse—exhibitionism, voyeurism, pornography, verbal sexual propositions or harassment

2. Abusive conditions—unequal power relationship
   a. Large age or maturational advantage over the child
   b. Abuser has position of authority or is child's caretaker
   c. Activities carried out using force or trickery

Child Molester—A significantly older person whose conscious sexual interests and other sexual behaviors are directed either partially or exclusively towards prepubertal children —a psychological as opposed to physiological disorder. Some characteristics:

1. Positive emotional investment in the child

2. Establishes ongoing relationship extending beyond sexual relationship
3. Psychologically harms the child, not physically
4. Non-violent
5. <u>Not a mental disorder</u> (Groth 1982)

Fixated Child Molester—
1. Undeveloped sociosexuality
2. Children are primary or exclusive objects of sexual interests
3. Any sexual contact with same age subject situational only, and does not replace desire for children (Groth 1982)

Regressed Child Molester—Cross-generational sexual activity precipitated by stressful situation with age mates, or coping with life in general (Groth 1982).

Diocesan priest—Diocesan clergy, or secular clergy as they are sometimes called, are priests or deacons who fall under the jurisdiction of the diocesan bishop in a geographical region.

Ephebophilia—Sexual activity, whether physical or otherwise, with a postpubescent or adolescent child or children.

Hierarchy—Governing body of the church: Pope, Cardinals, Provincials, Archbishops and Bishops.

Infantophilia—Sexual activity, whether physical or harassment, with a pre-pubescent infant, child or children generally age 0-5.

Ordination—The act of consecrating men to be sacred ministers for the worship of God and for the sanctification of all people.

Pedophilia—Sexual activity by an adult with a pre-pubescent child generally 13 years of age or younger.

Perpetrator—"to be guilty of; commit" (Webster 1996).

Predator—"one that preys, destroys or devours" (Webster 1996).

Religious Order Priest—A man who becomes an ordained member of a religious community, such as Jesuit, Franciscan, Redemptorist, Trappist, Holy Ghost, Dominican, and others. His superior would be a "provincial," the administrator of said society or order.

RICO—Racketeer Influenced and Corrupt Organizations (Act)

Roman Catholicism—The name of the church founded by Christ, whose members are named Catholic. This expression designates Christians who follow the Bishop of Rome, the Pope, who derives his supreme authority from the primacy of the Apostle Peter as Vicar of Christ.

Seminary—An ecclesiastical institute of learning whose sole purpose is to train young men for the reception of Holy Orders (ordination to the priesthood).

Sexual Offender—"person convicted of a sexual offense such as rape (sexual assault), unwanted sexual contact, or lewdness" (Gifis 1996).

U.S. Conference of Catholic Bishops (USCCB) Official body of United States bishops which focuses on internal concerns of the church, but has no authority over individual bishops.

Sociological Statistics:

Chi Square:

Measures the likelihood that the sample selected is representative of the population. The closer to .000, the more likely the response is not merely by chance. For instance, .001 indicates that the probability that the findings are merely by chance is one in 1,000, .0001 would be one in 10,000.

Gamma/Cramer's V: Measures the degree of association to produce trends. The higher the gamma 0-1, positive or negative, the closer the level of association.

References:

Babbie, Earl. 1995. *The Practice of Social Research.* Belmont, CA: Wadsworth.

Gifis, Steven H. 1996. *Law Dictionary.* Happauge, NY: Barron's.

Groth, Nichols, A., William F. Hobson and Thomas S. Gary. 1982. *The Child Molester: Clinical Observations.* Happauge, NY: Barron's.

Marshall, Gordon. 1994, 1996. *The Concise Oxford Dictionary of Sociology.* NY: Oxford U. Press.

The Official Catholic Directory. New Providence, NJ. P.J. Kenedy & Sons

Our Sunday Visitor's Catholic Encyclopedia. Huntington, IN: Our Sunday Visitor Pub.

1

National Federation of Priests' Council, 1993

M ost of us have lived our entire lives under the presumption that *Catholic priest = no sex*. Hundreds, perhaps thousands, of young men entered seminary in their early teens with the hope of becoming a priest. However, as time went on and they became sexually aware, they realized this was not the right life-choice for them, so they left and eventually married. Some even left within months of ordination, after six to ten years of seminary study. Still others became ordained, then felt something was missing in their lives so they left and became emotionally attached with someone on the outside, giving up the religious calling they believed they had in order to fulfill a separate calling to marriage and family.

There are different vows (or promises) in the priesthood regarding sex and marriage—chastity and celibacy—and the terms themselves may have different understandings. The *Catholic Encyclopedia* (Stravinskas 1991) defines "celibacy" and "chastity" as follows:

Celibacy: *The practice of perfect continence by priests and bishops meant to foster single-minded devotion to God and service in the ministry. According to the long-standing discipline of the Latin Rite Church, the rule of celibacy forbids marriage by priests and bishops, and it normally excludes married persons from ordination.*

Chastity: *The virtue which tempers, regulates and moderates our sexual desires, thoughts and actions. In marriage, chastity moderates desires for legitimate marital acts for the good of the family and of the union of the spouses; outside marriage, chastity restrains sexual desires, thoughts and actions in toto. Chastity is primarily a natural virtue, related to charity and justice because it inhibits the individual from regarding others as sexual objects; it therefore promotes respect for the dignity of other persons. Chastity prevents the Christian from demeaning the dignity of others and it enables one to treat others as true sons and daughters of God.*

A religious order priest (i.e., Jesuit, Dominican, Carmelite, Franciscan) makes a *vow* that he will be chaste. A diocesan priest only *promises* that he will not marry. The public has come to know that these different meanings and promises or vows have left openings for activity by priests that is deviant from the society's perception of *Catholic priest = no sex.*

It will also come as a surprise to some that there was a time when popes, bishops, and priests were married, and that the law of mandatory celibacy was not universally mandated for Latin Rite priests until the year 1139. Even more astounding is the fact that, while the Catholic institution explains celibacy as meant to "foster single-minded devotion to God and service in the ministry"—an undivided heart—the reality is that one of the main reasons the law was passed was because the church wanted the homes of deceased priests that were being bequeathed to their families. It is documented that in some instances, wives and children were even sold to slavery in order to be rid of them (Thomas 1986).

My curiosity in the phenomenon of sexual abuse by Roman Catholic clergy began in 1992 after an article appeared in *Vanity Fair,* (Bennetts 1991) that told of a Catholic priest whose identity and crimes were kept from the courts for two years because the district attorney was a friend of his. Then in 1993, the high-profile trial against Fr. James Porter, convicted of sexually abusing over fifty minors in the Fall River, Massachusetts, diocese, took place in Boston. A third trial, a class action suit, emerged in June 1993 in New Jersey. This time, the Catholic Church was being charged with federal racketeering (RICO): New Jersey victims had been sent across state lines to Rhode Island where the abuse took place (McCaffrey 1993).

Three weeks after the RICO case was filed, the Vatican released a statement that said, "Celibacy is not essential to the priesthood" (AP 7/18/93). I began to wonder: Why this Vatican statement and why now? Was there a causal relationship? Did the hierarchy fear what might be revealed in the U.S. courts? What did the church know that the public did not?

From 1992 to 1993, my involvement in church reform activities had been on the issues of churches closing and the shortage of priests. A personal experience, not being able to find a priest to visit my ailing mom, led to cursory research on mandatory celibacy in the priesthood, which evolved to founding a nonprofit lay organization, Celibacy Is the Issue (CITI), a free referral service of married priests to fill the spiritual needs of people who either cannot find priests or have been turned away by the church.

As president and founder of CITI Ministries/Rentapriest.com, I was subsequently invited to participate as a workshop guest speaker at the twenty-fifth anniversary conference of the National Federation of Priests Council (NFPC) in Chicago in May 1993. As a presenter, my badge allowed me entry into other workshops at the conference, one of which featuring clergy sexual abuse. I prepared the following report, but did not release it to the media until the following November when another major sexual abuse accusation was announced, this time against Joseph Cardinal Bernardin of Chicago, later exonerated:

November 13, 1993

Dear Ladies and Gentlemen of the Press:

I am a Catholic businesswoman, married and a grandmother, who because of the injustices I've seen regarding our married Catholic priests and the deprivation of the sacraments due to priestly shortages, founded an organization called Celibacy Is the Issue in February of 1992. In May of this year (1993), I served on a panel in a workshop on married priesthood at the National Federation of Priests Council Conference in Chicago.

As a speaker, my badge allowed me to enter other meetings at the conference, one of which was a clergy abuse workshop led by Fr. Canice Connors, head of St. Luke's Hospital in Suitland, Maryland, where most pedophile priests are sent for treatment. I took the following random notes of his remarks to over 300 priests in attendance, the first of its kind I was told.

The purpose of the workshop, as described by Fr. Connors, was to address the issue of clergy sexual abuse and attempt to obtain acceptance on the part of parish priests of "recovered" clergy back into respective parishes. An anonymous predator who had been in treatment 10 years for alcoholism and sexual abuse would bravely tell his story.

Fr. Connors' appeal was for sensitivity to St. Luke's "victim" against the "voyeurism of the laity and the press." He said, "Most priest predators are not pedophiles, but rather ephebophiles," describing the former as involving a pre-pubescent child, and having a "definite mental disorder, a lesion in the brain which does not inhibit the addiction."

He further said, ". . . an ephebophile (one who is sexually attracted to someone up to 19 years old) does respond to treatment and could be returned to normal ministry after 'recovery.'" He said that this addiction is due to "immaturity being encouraged in seminaries. Seminarians are told to not look into a woman's eyes—beware of (the) feminine. The feeling then becomes one of 'if girls are off limits, maybe boys are OK.'"

According to Fr. Connors, "What blew Newfoundland apart (the first major scandal in North America) was not so much the pedophile problem as the political problem with the bishop." The bishop had apparently negotiated a 7:30 am trial with the judge to keep it out of the press. The attorney on the case sensed extreme injustice, collusion between the church and the court, and reopened the case two years later—this time against the institution because of the dishonesty involved. Fr. Connors further commented, "How unfortunate it was that the Canadian bishops were not dealing with the truth and instead allowed fear and anxiety to rule, strategizing instead on how to deny, which only magnified the secrecy."

An anonymous priest in recovery 10 years for alcohol and sex addiction then spoke. (My heart went out to this fragile-looking destroyed soul.) He had been an "alcoholic for 18 years—lived in isolation—needed human contact." He "was cruising for anonymous sex." He said he "used bad judgment." He "chose youngsters in teenage years." He was "filled with devastation and shame and wondered who the monster in the mirror was." He said his addiction was "not fun, nor fulfilling."

When he first went to St. Luke's, he thought he "was an insane man with no hope, but that they offered hope and help." He "took (the) 12-step program." During his "addiction," he "had asked for psychological and medical help and was told there was none."

When Fr. Connors returned to the podium, he said, "For the sake of the Gospel, these brothers who can, should be reassigned. It is a shame these recovered priests are not invited back into ministry." (This priest was very frail, too fragile I felt to perform active ministry.)

Connors indicated that pedophilia cases are becoming public (1993) in New Zealand, Australia, Africa, Ireland, England, Holland and France, and that St. Luke's was training therapists to deal with them at the time of the conference. "Denial is a big part of the addiction," said Connors. "It's taken the church a long time to deal with sexual abuse." (The seminar was held at a time when the church [hierarchy] was still telling the public, as noted below, that this was "strictly an American problem.")

Fr. Connors then said, "Tighten your seatbelts. Accusations by adult women are next. And it is expected many priests will die of AIDS over the next five years." [See Thomas, Kansas City Star 1/29/00]

I had not intended to make this information public for the purpose of another sensationalistic press story. However, I decided to speak out for several reasons: the apparent denials and cover-ups which continue to occur, as reported by SNAP (Survivors Network of those Abused by Priests) who now estimate 100,000 U.S. victims, the accusations by Pope John Paul II that this is only an "American problem" (Time July 5, 1993— two months after the above seminar took place) and a recent article in the American Catholic Northeast featuring priest/psychiatrist Rev. Dr. James Gill, in which he states, "There is no conclusive evidence that celibacy increases the incidence of pedophilia."

During the question/answer period at the end of Fr. Connors' talk, I suggested that a scientific study be done to see if there is any connection between mandatory celibacy and sexual abuse since there has never been one, even though the church claims there is no connection. Fr. Connors' answer was that it "would be a waste of time and money." My feeling is if they are so sure, then why don't they disprove that it is connected? The July 2, 1993, issue of National Catholic Reporter reported that when a Canadian Ad Hoc Committee on Child Abuse was named to study the

*problem and issue its recommendations, the Canadian Bishops
gave "specific instructions not to study the nature and causes of
sexual abuse" (Fraze: 3).*

Sincerely,
Louise Haggett

No one acknowledged receiving my letter, and to my knowledge, this report was never published. It became apparent to me that clergy sexual abuse was still going on, and that the media was aware of it. Most stories on the abuse, if reported at all, remained buried in local news. The only news articles printed nationally seemed to appear in *National Catholic Reporter*, an independent Catholic newspaper to which I had subscribed in 1992.

Having witnessed the lack of response from the media and knowing that the bishops were discouraging causal research (Fraze ibid.), I felt compelled to get more deeply involved. From 1993 on, I tried to engage various Church reform organizations (over thirty) with more experience in church issues to join me in conducting research. No one would listen, although a few individuals provided encouragement.

One organization forced me to sign a document promising I would not link my own married priest reform work with the research. The document stipulated, however, that if the findings were significant, they would be permitted to publish them for their own benefit (letter on file). I was told I had "no right" to do the research. I later cancelled this agreement, and since the 2002 abuse revelations, this and other such organizations have made clergy sexual abuse part of their own agenda.

Realizing that I would have to do the research on my own, in the fall of 1996—at age fifty-five and with my husband's support—I quit my full-time job and enrolled again as a college student in order to learn the methodology of scientific research. I needed to get to the root of the observations I had made during the previous four years. My hypothesis was that, while some were attempting to link clergy sexual abuse with general population abuse or even abuse in other denominational religions, Roman Catholic clergy sexual abuse had unique characteristics.

The Bingo Report is the first published report of my research regarding the question, Is mandatory celibacy in the Catholic priesthood connected to Roman Catholic clergy sexual abuse?

The outline of this book is as follows:

Chapter 2—Updating a prior study of priests and their vows in the climate of clergy sexual abuse.

Chapter 3—Study of adolescent victims of clergy sexual abuse

Chapter 4—Study of adult victims of clergy sexual abuse

Chapter 5—Church reaction

Chapter 6—Literary Study conducted by me after reviewing and combining findings from the updated priest study and the victim studies.

Chapter 7—Conclusion

Chapter 8—How much does the church know?

A demonstrable link exists between mandatory celibacy and clergy sexual abuse. Sexual abuse by Roman Catholic clergy is different from sexual abuse by other populations in almost every aspect of the victim/perpetrator profiles and characteristics, differences that can only be seen by segregating respective demographics and other specifics from general population abuse.

These studies were conducted according to sociological standards and are reported as an academic paper in order to protect their integrity. The report, however, is written mostly in "layperson's" language. The information contained herein is so significant that it needs to be understood by a wide audience, not only by academics. A glossary and footnotes explain some of the scientific terminology that is being used. Religious terms are also explained.

Bibliography

Bennetts, Leslie. 1991. Unholy Acts. *Vanity Fair,* December.

Bonnike, Frank J., James Gower and Louise Haggett. 1993. "The Movement, the Ministries & the Methods." Workshop presented at the 25th Annual National Federation of Priests Council (NFPC) Convention & House of Delegates. Chicago, IL, May 3–7.

Connors, Fr. Canice. 1993. "The Issue of Sexual Misconduct & the Clergy." Workshop presented at the 25th Annual National Federation of Priests Council (NFPC) Convention & House of Delegates. Chicago, IL, May 3–7.

Fraze, Barb. 1993. "Canadian Bishops move vigorously on sex abuse problems." *National Catholic Reporter,* July 3.

Gill, Fr. James. 1993. "Human Sexuality, the Priesthood, and a Mature Laity." *The American Catholic Northeast,* October.

Haggett, Louise. 1999. "Is a Sexual Abusing Roman Catholic Priest a Pedophile? The Case for Ephebophilia." Paper presented at the Society for the Scientific Study of Religion and Religious Research Association Conference. Boston, MA, November 5–7.

_____. 2000. "Is a Sexual Abusing Roman Catholic Priest a Pedophile? The Case for Ephebophilia." Paper presented at the 70th Annual Meeting of the Eastern Sociological Society. Baltimore, MD, March 2–5.

Haggett, Louise, Tara Hanson and Megan Solo. 1997. "What Factors Contribute to Catholic Priests Breaking Their Vows of Celibacy/Chastity?" Unpublished.

McCaffrey, Joseph D., Monica Maske. 1993. "3 Men Sue South Jersey Priest for Sex Abuse." *The Star-Ledger,* June 11.

New York Times. 1993. "Pope: Celibacy Is Not Essential to the Priesthood." July 18.

Ostling, Richard N. 1993. "Sex and the Single Priest." *Time,* July 5.

Stravinskas, Rev. Peter M. J. 1991. *Our Sunday Visitor's Catholic Encyclopedia.* Huntington, IN: Our Sunday Visitor Publishing.

Thomas, Gordon. 1986. *Desire and Denial: celibacy and the church.* Boston: Little, Brown.

Thomas, Judy. 2000. "Report Explores AIDS, Priests." *Associated Press in Kansas City Star,* January 29. (http://www.kcstar.com/item/pages/home.pat,local/37743133.129.,HTML). Retrieved January 30, 2000.

Winter Report, The. 1990. Archdiocese of St. John's. Newfoundland, Canada, 36.

2

The Priest Study

Updating a Prior Study of Priests and Their Vows in the Climate of Clergy Sexual Abuse [1]

T he first Priest Study was conducted by a team of sociology students at Framingham State College during 1996–1997 under the direction of Dr. Marian Cohen. Though it was an original study, the Social Methods course dictated the use of a specific social theory from which to make comparisons in our paper. After much debate between the *learning theory* and other social theories such as *conflict,*[2] *anomie,*[3] or *control,*[4] the study team chose the *learning theory* (Simmel 1903, 1995). We were curious as to whether factors in

---

[1] Chapter 2 reassesses an earlier study conducted in 1997 by a team of college students at Framingham State College in Massachusetts: Louise Haggett, Tara Hanson and Megan Solo. The original study was entitled, "What Factors Contribute to Catholic Priests Breaking Their Vows of Celibacy/Chastity?" with an N=factor of seventy. The 2004 version was recalculated to include the seven responses that arrived after the 1997 deadline and was written in the climate of the Roman Catholic clergy sexual abuse that became widely known in January, 2002 via the *Boston Globe*.

[2] Conflict theory is about "power," emphasized by the importance of self-interest over norms and values.

[3] Anomie theory is confusion resulting from an absence, breakdown, and/or conflict over norms in society.

[4] Control theory, more commonly known as "social control," is an attempt to identify the techniques of control that may be employed in society. Source: *The Concise Oxford Dictionary of Sociology* (Marshall, 1994).

breaking the vows or promise of celibacy or chastity could be attributed to priests' societal socialization prior to seminary or whether it
was a result of the subculture in the priesthood.

The basis for the *learning theory* follows, after which is presented
the methodology, along with the results, summary, and conclusion
from a 2004 perspective. The detailed findings and statistical tables
with any significant measurements of association or probability used
in quantitative research are included at the end of Chapter 2 for those
who wish to review them.

Priest Study Abstract

The original study sought to learn what factors may have contributed
to Roman Catholic priests ("priests") breaking their vows/promises
(hereinafter referred to as "vows") of celibacy (no marriage) and/or
chastity (no sex). The socialization process between cultures and subcultures was analyzed to determine if conflict can result among groups
that are socialized in both—culture and subculture—especially if
some of the norms in each are different. According to *The Concise
Oxford Dictionary of Sociology*, the word "culture" is "an anthropological idea based on the definition provided by Edward Tylor in 1871 to
mean knowledge, belief, art, morals, law and custom within a society"
(104). "Subcultures are distinct from the larger culture, but may borrow some of its symbols, values and beliefs. The concept is widely
used in the sociology of deviance" (519). The dictionary also explains
that organizational subcultures may set up their own "values, norms,
and patterns of action that characterize social relationships within a
formal organization" (371).

Roman Catholic priests were once nurtured in secular society and
then they committed to celibacy on their path to ordination in the
priesthood. Which learned behavior prevailed, the earlier socialization
in the societal environment or the seminary/priesthood lifestyle?
Did these patterns lead to conflicts? If so, did these conflicts result in
deviant behavior[5] (different from norm) by some? The hypothesis

---

[5] Deviant behavior: Deviance as a pattern of norm violation.

tested among our target sample of priests was to question socialization patterns. The conclusions of our study indicated that while conflict can exist among groups belonging to two cultures, the conflict that exists among priests is multifaceted, with some common denominators relating to the length of time they have been in the priesthood, interpreted to mean how long they live in a celibate lifestyle. In our reassessment of the 1997 Priest Study (Haggett, Hanson and Solo), new concepts emerged regarding intense loneliness that is experienced by some priests living a celibate lifestyle, as well as church response to deviant behavior by priests, areas that were more closely examined in light of the clergy abuse revelations. Honoring vows continues to be important to most priests, but our findings suggest that the reality of honoring their vows appears for many to be an emotional struggle and that the breaking of vows is more influenced by the subculture of the priesthood than secular society.

The Learning Theory[6]

Socialization takes place as a result of behavior learned within cultures and subcultures. It can begin as early as in the teaching of American customs at the same time as ethnic customs to young children, subcultures within the American society. Socialization may differ among groups within these cultures and subcultures depending on what norms are relevant to or valued by them. A behavior, therefore, may be considered normative or deviant (different from the norm), depending on the group that is viewing or judging the behavior because norms learned within a society do not necessarily coincide with norms learned within a subculture of the same society.

Ronald Akers (1985) wrote that deviance results from learning definitions that portray certain conduct as acceptable by some even though it may be considered unacceptable by others. A simple example of this would be physical abuse that is learned as a form of discipline. What children witness in the home—a parent abusing another parent and/or children—can send a message that this method

---

[6] The learning theory presented here was partially developed by Haggett et al. (1997).

is appropriate for resolving domestic issues. Thus, physical abuse may be learned within the family subculture even though the larger society professes that physical abuse is wrong.

People in a subculture behave in ways that may be standard in their immediate group but not necessarily in society at large. This contrast may cause conflict for individuals who have been socialized in one culture, then experience a different socialization process in another culture or subculture. The premise is that the more we are exposed to the influence of a particular group, the more our own patterns of behavior may change to conform, no matter what we learned previously. If people can collectively act as a group, their behavior begins to coincide with the group.

According to Herbert Blumer (1969), role-taking by groups is based on the action of other groups, social structures, and cultural directives. Thus, individual actions and those of other social structures can mirror one another. "The concept of subculture has served well for those who hold the idea that culture mirrors society. It has allowed them to assert that groups that regularly deviate from societal norms are subculture conformists" (Peterson, 1979:147). At the same time, however, "the subcultural idea has deflected researchers in this tradition from challenging the conception of a dominant culture mirrored by society" (Fischer 1975 in Peterson, 1979:147).

College students are a recent good example of this theory. For instance, the foot fashion fad among American college students during the early 2000s was to wear "flip-flops," a beach-type sandal, instead of shoes on a year-round basis, while the rest of the secular world—at least in the United States—continued to wear regular footwear. In 2005, the fad caught on and major retailers began featuring accessory departments apart from the shoe department that display "flip-flops" in every color and design imaginable, and everyone is buying them. College students at first were subculture conformists, now society is mirroring the subculture.

The social structure of the Catholic Church is created, maintained, and changed through interactive processes. In the article

"Religion and Role Identity," religious norm adherence is discussed as the degree to which an individual adheres to the normative expectation of his or her religious group (Wimberley 1989). This adherence depends on one's religious salience or "the extent to which the religious identity is dominant among other identities" (130). The question becomes, "To what extent will one be willing to violate other types of norms?" Does a priest see himself as a religious being before he sees himself as a sexual being?

Norms learned within the Latin Rite of the church and society at large may contradict each other. This may have a significant impact on whether or not priests adhere to the vow of celibacy and chastity. Priests make a conscious choice to enter the religious environment. In doing so, they have to promise or vow that they will remain celibate and chaste, depending on whether they become diocesan or religious order priests, as explained in chapter 1.

Priests are taught and may likely believe (at least at the beginning of their training) that they would be more effective in their ministry as celibates. Because of their deep desire or divine calling to be priests, they may agree to these disciplines in order to be ordained. While priests learn that it is not acceptable to break their vows regarding sexuality, the larger society teaches them that it is normal to be sexual beings. As a result, priests may experience conflict between their ministry and the vows they took, their own needs, or what they witness in society as well as within the Catholic institutional subculture.

Negotiations for roles and rules occur also within organizational structures, though often this may yield only system adjustment, not radical change (Musolf 1992:184). There may be an underlying acceptance of deviance (breaking of vows) in the Catholic Church as long as priests do not marry or create a public scandal (Kennedy 1993:5). The reconciliation of the conflict created in the mind of an individual priest may occur if he feels that his behavior has been condoned in both cultures. If there is any church discipline, it may not be sufficient to prevent deviance; and until recently, sexual deviance among priests if exposed was typically excused by the general public as an isolated instance[7]. In fact, a double standard existed regarding public reaction to a priest offender versus a neighbor down the street.

The learning theory from the perspective of Edwin H. Sutherland (1992) accounts well for the cause of deviance. Sutherland argues that deviant behavior is a consequence of normative conflict, or conflict from learning opposing sets of norms. He explains that normative conflict results in deviant behavior through association or the learned behavior from primary contact groups.

Factors contributing to the breaking of vows within the priesthood may be relative to socialization that occurs in two different environments. Norm adherence may reflect forces arising from the combination of the normative expectation of the religious culture and the larger social environment, in addition to the individual priest's own moral values (Wimberley 1989:137). When opposing identities or norms call for different behaviors, the behavior that the person relates to the most will take precedence. However, because there is conflict when acting against what is expected in a culture or society, the person may need his peers to legitimize and redefine his behavior as appropriate. This is also supported by Tomasello, Kruger and Ratner (1993), who explain that "Once a practice is begun by some members of a culture, others acquire it relatively faithfully but then modify it as needed (495)." In order for modification of behavior to occur on a social level or within a group, the process of learning from others needs to occur. In terms of the priesthood, the legitimization of the deviant behavior can occur when peers look the other way or engage in the same activity, and/or if there is no discipline from the superiors.

As of 1996, there had been little research comparing the subculture of the Catholic priesthood to secular society even though the Catholic institution is a large and important subculture of society. The messages that priests receive from their own subculture regarding their sexuality may be different from the beliefs of society at large in the United States. Much has been reported in secular media regarding the sexual misbehavior among this supposedly chaste group, creating particular concern

---

[7] It has become common knowledge that this practice continued until the 2002 revelations, perhaps because of disbelief by the public.

because the church as an institution and its priests teach moral values. The 1997 study reviewed in this chapter, which asks what factors from a priest's perspective might contribute to priests breaking the vow of celibacy/chastity, is significant because its uniqueness may open up additional doors of research in other isolated subcultures such as female religious orders, the military and prison institutions.

Methodology

Our study population was the Roman Catholic, Latin Rite priesthood in the United States, of which there were 49,009 in 1995 (The Official Catholic Directory 1996). We chose the priesthood population because of the high incidence of sexual misbehavior in the Catholic institution already made public by 1996, and because no sexual abuse studies were found from a sociological perspective that isolated any group of people where mandatory celibacy is a prerequisite to membership, and where celibacy and sexual deviance could be combined as variables. Hence, this is an original study.

A self-administered survey questionnaire was used to allow for anonymity and confidentiality. The instrument contained many sensitive questions that we felt priests would be more willing to answer without an interviewer present. We opted not to code the instruments or envelopes in order to maintain confidentiality for the respondents. The cover letter explained that the respective priests' names had been selected randomly from a total population of priests eligible for our study, thus covering a broader area than we would have been able to achieve had we been limited to personal interviews. The questionnaire was mailed to 248 priests from the 1996 edition of *The Official Catholic Directory* (Kenedy).

The data-gathering instrument included several types of questions. The demographic questions were open-ended: *how many years a priest, age of entry into seminary, number of years in present assignment, number of assignments in the past ten years*, and *dating history prior to seminary entry*. The majority of the other questions were closed-ended, seven using the Likert Scale (strongly agree to strongly disagree). Three semantic differential questions with possible responses ranging from "frequently" to "never" were asked regarding *dating, disciplining of priests* by the church, and whether or not priests were *tempted to break their vows.* The open-ended questions asked for additional factors that contribute to priests' *adhering to* or *breaking* their vows of chastity/celibacy.

The response rate was 31.0 percent (N=77 of 248). The relevance of our study was enhanced by the fact that 72 out of the 77 (93.5 percent) respondents added comments throughout and/or at the end of the study and a few signed their names even though this was a confidential study. There were patterns (minimum 10 percent response rate) of positive experiences recorded by priests as well as patterns of frustrations with church policy, particularly regarding mandatory celibacy. Of particular significance were the high percentages of write-in responses to open-ended questions: *other factors* regarding *adherence to,* or *breaking of,* a vow (in questions 13 and 23). For instance, almost 60 percent of those who responded to *what other factors contribute to priests breaking their vow of celibacy/chastity* indicated "loneliness" (lack of intimacy, marriage, etc.) as the reason. Another significant instance was a write-in of the words *only when there is public knowledge* by nearly 10 percent of total priests who responded to *how often* the church disciplines priests who break a vow (question 17). Among respondents who said that *priests break vows,* 100 percent indicated that the church disciplines *only when there is public knowledge*; 20 percent of the respondents who were non-committal when asked if the church disciplines also indicated that discipline took place *only when there is public knowledge.*

Our target sample was sufficiently large and heterogeneous so that a survey methodology allowed us to obtain a significant amount of information about them in a relatively short period of time. We ensured validity by asking the respondents both questions that they knew how to answer and in which they had an interest.

There was intersubjectivity among the research team: members representing different views at the outset of the study regarding the hypothesis, as well as different religions influencing some of the questions asked. When researchers have different or opposing views about a scientific project, it helps make these observers more objective and gives more credence to their work. Hence, the research team helped make the study and its findings "objectively true."

Our respondents were male, since the total priest population is male. Demographics of our respondents are as follows:

Table 2.1 Demographics of Priest Respondents		
How many years a priest?	**Number**	**Percent***
0–10 years	6	8%
11–20 years	17	22%
21–30 years	16	21%
31–40 years	21	27%
41+ years	17	22%
Age entered into seminary:		
13–15 years old	19	25%
16–19 years old	32	42%
20–29 years old	21	27%
30+ years old	5	6%
Dated prior to seminary:		
Yes	53	69%
No	24	31%
Type of Priest**		
Diocesan	52	67%
Religious order	25	33%
How long in present assignment		
0–4 years	31	42%
5–10 years	25	34%
11+ years	18	24%
3	no response	
Number of assignments in the past 10 years		
1–2	49	69%
3–4	17	24%
5–10	5	7%
6	no response	

* percentages rounded off

** The actual priest census in the 1996 Catholic Directory was 66.1 percent diocesan 33.9 percent Religious Order. Other total population demographic comparisons are not available.

The SPSS (Statistical Package for Social Sciences) computer program for Microsoft©Windows, Version 10.0 was used to tabulate the responses. We measured frequencies, correlations (including intercorrelations), and cross-tabulations among all variables.

In light of new information regarding clergy sexual abuse claims and the church's complicity in relation to these abuses, the raw data and the original findings were reexamined in 2004. Hence, the results, summary, and conclusion have a 2004 perspective.

Results

There were statistically significant relationships between certain variables and the total priest population sample, as well as in cross-tabulations within specific demographics. Worthy of note was the dichotomy that existed in responses between the *attitude* of respondents toward adhering to in contrast with their *behavior* regarding breaking their vows. While they said they believed one thing, the action reported contradicted what they said they believed.

Examples appear in the General Response Table 2.2. For instance, *Do you adhere to your vows?* received an 86.8 percent affirmative response, yet when asked, *Do you occasionally not adhere?* 43.1 percent said yes. Notice also the large-scale inconsistencies, especially the Neither Agree nor Disagree (NAD) column between Table 2.20 and Table 2.21 under Age of Entry: *Do priests have sexual needs? Do priests break vows because of sexual needs?* These are just two of the many contradictions that can be viewed in both the general table (2.2) and even more significant among the cross-tabulations that appear in the detailed findings in Appendix A at the end of chapter 2.

Some of the *attitude and behavior* tables included in Appendix A may not appear to be significant in terms of measurement of association (relationship to one another), but help to illustrate the disparity between *attitude* and *behavior* among the responses.

The Likert Scale is represented as SA, A, NAD, D, and SD for *Strongly Agree, Agree, Neither Agree nor Disagree, Disagree,* and *Strongly Disagree.* NAD is sometimes written as "noncommittal" in the text; this usage means that the respondents checked *Neither Agree nor Disagree.*

Total Sample Findings

Table 2.2 General Responses from Total Priest Sample (N=77)

Variable	Strongly Agree	Agree	Neither Agree /disagree	Disagree	Strongly disagree
Honoring Vow Important	82.4 %	16.2 %	1.4 %	0.0 %	0.0 %
Adhere b/c Important	53.3 %	38.7 %	5.3 %	2.7 %	0.0 %
Believe in Divine Retribution	12.5 %	19.4 %	19.4 %	31.9 %	16.7 %
Adhere b/c Belief	4.2 %	9.7 %	19.4 %	34.7 %	31.9 %

Other Factors for Adhering	Devotion to Ministry	Faithful to Promise	Reputation	Other
	69.6%	25.0 %	3.6 %	1.8 %

Variable	Strongly Agree	Agree	Neither Agree /Disagree	Disagree	Strongly Disagree
Priests Break Vows	42.7 %	50.6 %	6.7 %	0.0 %	0.0 %
Church Acknowledges Priests Break Vows	33.8 %	60.6 %	4.2 %	1.4 %	0.0 %
Church Disciplines	10.8 %	44.6 %	32.3 %	10.8 %	1.5 %

How Often Does Church Discipline *Write in	Frequently	Occasionally	Not often	Never	Public Knowledge only
	15.4%	55.8 %	17.3 %	1.9 %	9.6 %

Variable	Strongly Agree	Agree	Neither Agree /Disagree	Disagree Strongly	Disagree
Believe in Sexual Freedom in Society	48.6 %	43.2 %	2.7 %	4.1 %	1.4 %
Break Vows b/c Sexual Freedom	17.6 %	50.0 %	13.2 %	17.6 %	1.5 %
People Have Sex Needs	36.0 %	60.0 %	1.3 %	1.3 %	1.3 %
Priests Have Sex Needs	39.7 %	54.8 %	4.1 %	1.4 %	0.0 %
Break Vows/Sex Needs	10.4 %	43.3 %	29.9 %	9.0 %	7.5 %

Other Factors for Breaking Vows	Loneliness	Weakness	Lack of Prayer	Church Issues	Substance Abuse	Societal Pressures	Other
	59.3 %	16.9 %	6.8 %	6.8 %	6.8 %	1.7 %	1.7 %

Variable	Yes	No
Do You Adhere?	86.8 %	13.2%
Do You Occasionally Not Adhere?	43.1 %	56.9 %

Tempted to Break Vow?	Frequently	Occasionally	Not Often	Never
	15.8 %	50.0 %	21.1 %	13.2 %

	Yes	No
Believe in Optional Celibacy?	69.9 %	30.1 %
Should Priests Marry?	86.5 %	13.5 %

- Respondents almost unanimously (98.6 percent) said they believe that honoring vows is important, and 92 percent said priests adhere to their vows because of the importance of honoring vows.
- Less than one-third of priest respondents said they believe it is a sin to break their vow. Only 13.9 percent said they adhere to their vows because it is a sin to break their vows. Almost 20 percent were noncommittal.

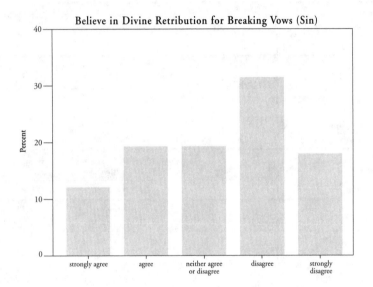

Believe in Divine Retribution for Breaking Vows (Sin)

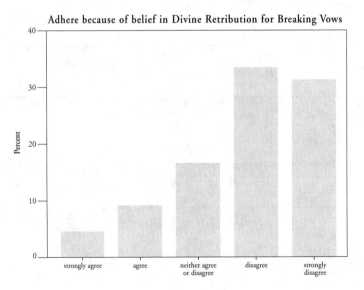

Adhere because of belief in Divine Retribution for Breaking Vows

- When asked what other factors contribute to adhering to their vows, an open-ended question, they wrote in:
  - 69.6 percent Devotion to ministry
  - 25.0 percent Faithful to promise of celibacy/chastity
  - 3.6 percent Reputation
  - 1.8 percent Other

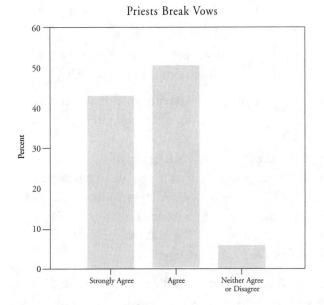

Priests Break Vows

- 93.3 percent agreed that priests break vows, and 6.7 percent were noncommittal.
- 94.4 percent said the church acknowledges the breaking of vows, but 40 percent fewer or 55.4 percent said the church disciplines the breaking of vows.
- When asked *how often* the church disciplines the breaking of vows, 15.4 percent said *frequently* and 55.8 percent said *occasionally*. Another 28.8 percent said *not often, never,* or *only when it becomes public knowledge*. If we add to the 28.8 percentage, those among the total population who did not respond to the above *acknowledge* or *discipline* questions, which we interpret to mean *no/never*, it brings the percentage up to 43.4 percent of

respondents who said (or implied) *not often, never,* or **wrote in** *only when it becomes public knowledge.*

- 91.8 percent of the respondents said they believe there is sexual freedom in society, but one-third fewer (67.6 percent) were willing to blame sexual freedom in society for priests breaking their vows.

- 94.5 percent said they believe that priests have sexual needs, but 40 percent fewer (53.7 percent) said they believe that priests break their vows because of sexual needs.

- When asked what other factors contribute to *breaking* their vows, an open-ended question, they responded:

  - 59.3 percent   Loneliness, lack of intimacy, marriage and family
  - 16.9 percent   Weakness
  - 6.8 percent   Lack of prayer
  - 6.8 percent   Frustrated with church policies regarding mandatory celibacy
  - 6.8 percent   Substance abuse
  - 1.7 percent   Societal pressures
  - 1.7 percent   Other

- While 86.6 percent said they adhere to their vows, 43.1 percent said they break their vows occasionally. This response is typical of many of the statistics in the Priest Study that may appear to be wrong. That is not the case. One proofreader of this book wrote, "How can this be? I don't smoke cigarettes, but I have three or four a day, seems to be a logical parallel. Am I missing something?" Our interpretation of the many contradictory responses is that priests are conflicted, perhaps because they are told one thing, they witness another, their superiors seem to have a blind eye to the deviance, so they think it is okay to break their vows.

- 69.9 percent said they believe in optional celibacy, yet 86.5 percent say that priests should be allowed to marry, essentially the same question producing inconsistent responses.

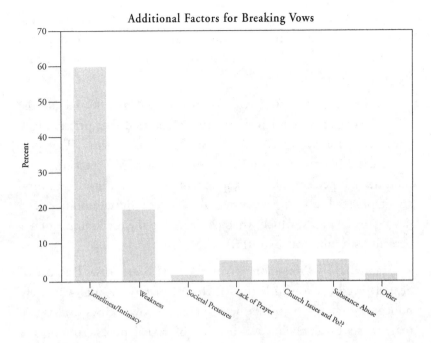

Additional Factors for Breaking Vows

Statistical Highlights

Below are statistical highlights from a chi square analysis[8] that indicated significant differences among cross tabulations. A more comprehensive report on the findings along with respective tables appears at the end of chapter 2.

Table 2.4—Years in Priesthood/Honoring Vows-Adhere: The longer priests remain in the priesthood, the more they said they adhere to their vows because of the importance of honoring vows. The expectation was that a newly-ordained priest, having just made his vows, would have been more likely to adhere the most. The opposite was true. This is considered an inverse relationship (p<.001).

[8] Chi Square is a measurement of the likelihood that the sample selected is representative of the population. The closer to .000, the more likely the response is not merely by chance. For instance, .001 indicates that the probability that these findings are merely by chance is one in 1,000; .0001, one in 10,000.

Table 2.30—# Assignments in 10 Years/Believe there is Sexual Freedom in Society: The more times a priest was moved from parish to parish in 10 years, the less he believed that there is sexual freedom in society (p<.001).

Table 2.33—Priests Break Vows/Priests Have Sexual Needs: 63.3 percent of respondents who strongly agreed that priests break vows also strongly agreed that priests have sexual needs. This percentage (63.3 percent) against the total sample of 39.7 percent is significant. 25 percent of the respondents who were noncommittal about priests breaking vows were also noncommittal about priests having sexual needs, which when compared to the total sample of 4.1 percent, is significant (p<.001).

Table 2.34—Priests Break Vows/Priests Break Vows Because of Sexual Needs: Two-thirds (66.7 percent) of respondents who were noncommittal about priests breaking their vows strongly disagree that priests break their vows because of sexual needs. Among the total priest sample: 7.5 percent (p<.001).

Table 2.35—Priests Break Vows/Church Acknowledges the Breaking of Vows: Nearly all (94.3 percent) who admitted that priests break vows said the church acknowledges that priests break vows; 71.9 percent strongly agreed. Among the total priest sample: 33.8 percent (p<.0001).

Table 2.37—Priests Break Vows/How Often Does the Church Discipline? All (100 percent) of the respondents who were noncommittal about priests breaking vows said that discipline only happens when there is public knowledge. As previously indicated *public knowledge* was a write-in response; it was not listed as an option on the survey instrument (p<.0001).

Table 2.39—Church Disciplines/How Often Does the Church Discipline? 100 percent of the respondents who were noncommittal about whether or not the church *disciplines* the breaking of vows said that the discipline takes place only when there is *public knowledge* (a write-in response) of the breaking of vows (p<.001).

Summary—2004

Our findings were significant and/or relational in several instances and nonrelational in others. Prior to undertaking our study, we anticipated a measurable variation in attitudes and behaviors among priests regarding their vows based on their degree of socialization—whether or not it made a difference if they entered the seminary before or after puberty, whether or not they dated prior to entry, whether or not the length of stay would solidify their vocation, whether or not they lived in community with other priests or in a parish house in a more public environment, the length of assignment they had, and the number of times they were moved from assignment to assignment in the previous 10 years.

We discovered that *the length of time a priest was in the priesthood made more of an impact on his attitude and behavior than any other factor.* Priests in the priesthood 21–30 years consistently responded differently from the other categories within the demographic category of *number of years in the priesthood.* These statistics stood out as either very high or very low in comparison with other categories within the same demographic, indicating that there are issues that affect priests based on the length of time they serve in the priesthood, more than any other factor. This is contrary to our original hypothesis, which was that the longer a priest remains in the priesthood, the more entrenched in the priesthood he becomes; and the more entrenched in the priesthood he becomes, the less likely he is to break his vow of celibacy/chastity.

We were surprised to find that newly ordained priests (0–10 years) responded almost identically to those in the priesthood 21–30 years in a few of the questions: under SA in *believe in divine retribution for the breaking of vows,* and *adhere because of belief in divine retribution,* and in general in *priests break vows because of sexual freedom in secular society.* In the question *Do you adhere?* the newly ordained priests' responses were similar to those in the priesthood 41+ years. In examining the demographics more closely, we discovered that one-third of our respondents in the 0–10 years category were 30+ years old at age of entry. This would explain some of the similarities in responses to other older priests (i.e., in the priesthood 21 or more years). Seminary teachings may be different for, or have a different effect on, men who enter the seminary at a more mature level of psychosexuality than those who entered at 13 years of age.

Except for the above consideration and the sexual needs tables 2.20 and 2.21 as previously mentioned, *Age of Entry* was insignificant as an independent variable because all ages of entry were represented in one question or another. We would therefore argue that age of entry is not as significant as longevity in the priesthood in terms of conflicts that may arise regarding the factors included in the Priest Study. The same held true for the *Dating Prior to Seminary* or *Type of Priest* demographics.

In the *Type of Priest* category, religious order priests who by and large live in religious communities such as monasteries as opposed to parish houses among secular society responded more similarly to parish priests than we anticipated. That was also unexpected. Our hypothesis was that if priests lived in religious communities, their attitudes and behaviors would be different from diocesan (parish) priests whose lives had intertwined with the public on a daily basis and therefore might be more swayed by secular society. In our pre-study thinking, we were influenced by the following quote from a Vatican official in *Time*: "The church doesn't have a problem with sex. The world does (Ostling 1993:66)." Our data indicate, however, that it doesn't matter where priests live; they all experience the same phenomenon the longer they remain in the priesthood. The independent variable *How long have you been in your present assignment* also had little effect on responses.

The rate at which priests contradicted themselves or chose the noncommittal (NAD) response to specific questions is worthy of note. For the majority of questions regarding their *belief/attitude,* respondents gave a straightforward answer in either Strongly Agree or Agree, or Disagree or Strongly Disagree categories. However, when asked about their sexual behavior in relation to their *belief/attitude,* respondents were noncommittal (NAD) in double-digit percentages —some as high as 32.3 percent in the general responses or 100 percent in several cross-tabulations. This disparity was present in all questions that were two-part, attitude versus behavior, such as *divine retribution, sexual needs,* and *sexual freedom in secular society,* and also *church discipline* questions.

For instance, the questions regarding whether or not they *adhere to their vow, occasionally break it,* or are *tempted* to do so resulted in inconsistencies, as did the questions on *optional celibacy* versus *should priests be allowed to marry.* We anticipated that the latter two sets of percentages would mirror each other since optional celibacy and priests being allowed to marry mean the same thing. That was not the case.

When asked if they adhered to their own vows, 13.2 percent of the total sample said they did not. Among the individual demographics, however, we found that almost double the number (25.0 percent) of priests who entered the seminary between the ages of 16 and 19 admitted to not adhering to their vows (Table 2.24) and three times the number (40.0 percent) of priests with 5–10 assignments in 10 years admitted to not adhering to their vows (Table 2.32). These data suggest that a significant number of the 13.2 percent of priests who said they do not adhere came from these two categories.

In performing intercorrelations between the two independent variables, age of entry and number of assignments in 10 years, we discovered that 40 percent of priests with 5–10 assignments within a 10-year period entered the priesthood between the ages of 16 and 19, double the amount of any other age category. Among those in the priesthood 21–30 years (the most significant variable in our study), 60 percent entered between the ages of 16 and 19, the highest age of entry group within number of years in the priesthood.

There was a strong intercorrelation between *additional factors for adhering to the vows* and *priests break vows because of sexual needs*: 75.0 percent of priests who said that priests adhere to their vows in order to be faithful to their promise SA or A that priests break their vows because of sexual needs; 82.4 percent of those who said that *devotion to ministry* was the reason for adhering to their vows agreed or were noncommittal about priests breaking their vows because of sexual needs. *These results indicated a strong and widespread belief that sexual needs also dictate behavior among many priests.*

Other evidence that the ordained who agree to enforced celibacy break their vows because of sexual needs appears in a book entitled *The Priest: Celibate or Married* by Pierre Hermand (1965). In the section, *A permanent problem in the Church*, Hermand wrote,

> *It is well known that these habits [breaking vows] made their way into the pontifical court, especially in the fifteenth century under the pontificates of Sixtus IV (1471–1484), Innocent VIII (1484–1492) and Alexander (1492–1503). As early as 1414, seven hundred prostitutes had come to take up residence at Constance, on the occasion of the Council [of bishops] which was to meet there (35).*

The issue of loneliness was unforeseen. Almost 60 percent of those who responded to the question "What additional factors might contribute to the breaking of their vows?" wrote in *loneliness* either by itself or in conjunction with words like *lack of intimacy, marriage* and *family,* and/or *relationship.* Some added that breaking their vows had "more to do with lack of intimacy than just sex." This presents an opportunity for future studies among this celibate subculture of men who are forced to live a life alone and without a family.

The question of socialization had some significant results. Among the total sample, 91.8 percent believe there is sexual freedom in secular society. Yet, almost one-third fewer (67.6 percent) of the total sample believed that secular society influences the breaking of vows among priests. Among specific subgroups, however, both the newly ordained priests and priests with 21–30 years in the priesthood were split 50/50 regarding priests breaking their vows because of societal reasons.

While respondents said they are influenced by society in their attitude, our data indicate their behavior is not motivated by society.

The more assignments a priest had in a 10-year period, the less he agreed that there is sexual freedom in society.

When we ran an intercorrelation between number of assignments in 10 years and age of entry, we found that the percentages in 5–10 assignments were spread almost evenly among all ages of entry with the exception of 16 to 19 years old. We would interpret that to mean that the age of a new seminarian is not a factor in the breaking of vows as much as the length of time he remains in the priesthood.

Conclusion—2004

The object of our study was to see if socialization influenced the behavior of priests in regard to the vow of celibacy/chastity. In our exploration of the learning theory, we were curious as to which learning pattern from which culture would prevail: the secular culture where the priest respondents were first socialized or the church's subculture where socialization occurred later. For those who entered seminary at 13 years of age, psychosexual development or lack thereof was the dominant influence.

Our conclusion is that the subculture (the church environment) plays the more important role in the action of priests regarding their sexuality, more so than the earlier socialization that took place in their respective families and in society in general. The longer priests remain in the clerical subculture, the more influenced they are by the subculture. Our data indicate that the church's internal socialization of priests had more of an effect on the priests' behavior than "sexual freedom in secular society," as some might believe. We conclude that sexual deviance would be a learning experience for priests in the subculture of the priesthood and therefore believe that the learning theory was supported in this study.

This view is sustained by the responses to the secular society questions from populations whom we view as conflicted: those in the priesthood 21–30 years, those having 5–10 assignments within a 10-year period, and those who entered the seminary between the ages of

16 and 19, as well as the fact that only 1.7 percent among the total sample cited societal pressures as reasons for breaking their vows. The theory is further strengthened by the church discipline questions, especially those that dealt with *how often* discipline took place.

The strongest evidence we found is that the majority of priests:

1. Don't believe in divine retribution (a sin) for breaking their vows
2. Know overwhelmingly that other priests break their vows
3. Know overwhelmingly that the church acknowledges the breaking of vows
4. Indicate that the church disciplines only from occasionally to never—or only when there is public knowledge of the deviance, a fact not made public until at least 2002.

There was a high rate of response among priest respondents regarding whether or not they believe that "honoring vows is important," though the reality may be more difficult to achieve. We interpret the high rate of NAD responses to mean respondents who may have been embarrassed to admit that the church does not discipline, but did not want to lie. Otherwise, they would have said Strongly Agree or Agree.

The most shocking discovery in our findings, and one that was not made prior to the reassessment in 2004, was that it was not publicly known that there had been very little *internal* discipline over the past thirty or forty years for the breaking of vows. This finding is significant because it suggests that the lack of discipline would also be a learning experience for priests that sexual deviance will go unpunished until or unless there is public scandal. It shows that the subculture of the church is the ultimate influence regarding the socialization of priests with regard to sexual deviance.

Because of the many contradictory responses within the same questions between *attitude* and *behavior* of priests, we conclude that priests are internally conflicted about sexual issues. The conflicts may involve sexual deviance, the reporting or lack thereof, or perhaps other issues regarding morality since priests are presumed to be moral leaders.[9] The responses indicated that as priests, they know that the church does not practice what it preaches. Subsequent research might investigate the conflict theory among these men to determine what psychological consequences this conflict has had on them as individuals.

Priests are willing to communicate their views, demonstrated by the many write-in comments we received. This is supported by the front-page headline of the April 18, 1997, issue of *National Catholic Reporter* regarding priests with AIDS. It read, "Priests Finally Feel Free to Talk" (Schaeffer 1997:3). A confidential open-ended questionnaire utilizing the conflict or anomie theory may produce additional data that will provide an even better understanding of the phenomenon.

Bibliography

Akers, Ronald L. 1985. *Deviant Behavior: A Social Learning Perspective.* Belmont, CA: Wadsworth.

Associated Press. 1998. Pentagon Estimates Viagra Costs $50M. *The Union Leader.* Manchester, NH, October 3.

Blumer, Herbert. 1969. *Symbolic Interactionism: Perceptions and Method.* NJ: Prentice-Hall.

Fischer, David R. 1975, in Peterson, Richard A. (1979). "Revitalizing the Culture Concept." *1979 Annual Review of Sociology.*

Haggett, Louise, Tara Hanson and Megan Solo. 1996. "What Factors Contribute to Catholic Priests Breaking Their Vows of Celibacy/Chastity? Unpublished.

Hermand, Pierre. 1965. *The Priest: Celibate or Married.* Baltimore: Helicon. Original French title (1963): "Condition du Prête et marriage ou célibat?" Paris: Calmann-Levy.

Kennedy, Eugene. 1993. "Sex Abuse and Catholic Clerical Culture." *National Catholic Reporter,* March 19.

---

[9] That priests are known to be moral leaders is not a self-imposed notion. In his discussion on the theory of morality, Emil Durkheim wrote, "The commitment to the common morality must be learned in schools, when the teacher operates as the functional equivalent of the priest" (Durkheim in Turner, 1993:346).

Marshall, Gordon. 1996. *The Concise Oxford Dictionary of Sociology*. NY: Oxford U. Press.

Maslow, Abraham H. 1970. *Motivation and Personality.* NY: Harper & Row.

Musolf, Gil Richard. 1992. "Structure, Institutions, Power & Ideology: New Directions within Symbolic Interactionism. *Sociological Quarterly,* 33:184.

Official Catholic Directory, The, 1996. Edited by Kenedy, P.J. & Sons. New Providence, NJ: Reed.

Ostling, Richard N. 1991. "Handmaid or Feminist?" *Time,* December 30.

Powers, William T. 1973. *Behavior: The Control of Perception.* Chicago: Aldine.

Schaeffer, Pamela. 1997. "Breaking Silence: Priests with AIDS Are Eager to Talk." *National Catholic Reporter,* April 18.

Schoenherr, Richard and Lawrence Young. 1993. *Full Pews and Empty Altars.* Madison, WI: U. of Wis. Press.

Simmel, Georg. 1995, 1903. "The Web of Group Affiliations." *The Emergence of Sociological Theory,* edited by Serina Beauparlant. Belmont, CA: Wadsworth.

Sipe, A. W. Richard. 1990. *A Secret World: Sexuality and the Search for Celibacy.* NY: Brunner/Mazel.

————.1995. *Sex, Priests and Power: Anatomy of a Crisis.* NY: Brunner/Mazel.

Sutherland, Edwin H. 1992. "Sutherland's Theory: An Example of a Socialization Theory." *Sociology of Deviant Behavior,* edited by Marshall B. Clinard and Robert F. Meier. FL: Harcourt.

Stravinskas, Rev. Peter M.J. 1991. *Our Sunday Visitor's Catholic Encyclopedia.* Huntington, IN: Our Sunday Visitor Publishing.

Tomasello, Michael, Ann Cole Kruger, Hilary Horn Ratner. 1993. "Cultural Learning." *Behavioral and Brain Sciences,* 16:495–552.

Wimberley, Dale W. 1989. "Religion and Role Identity: A Structural Symbolic Interactionist's Conceptualization of Religiosity." *The Sociological Quarterly,* 30:130.

Appendix A

Detailed Findings

The following section reports on the findings that were significant among crosstabulations. As mentioned previously, some tables, though not statistically significant, are included to demonstrate the contradictory responses received in several instances among similar questions. Inconsistencies also appear between *attitude* questions and *behavior* questions (i.e., Tables 2.3 and 2.4).

The measurements used in these statistics include Chi Square, Gamma and Cramer's V. Chi Square is a measurement of the likelihood that the sample selected is representative of the study population. The closer to .000, the more likely the response is not merely by chance. For instance, the .001 indicates that the probability that these findings are merely by chance is one in 1,000 and .0001—one in 10,000. Gamma and Cramer's V measure the degree of association; the higher the gamma, between 0–1, the closer the level of association. Negative association refers to an inverse relationship—as one variable goes up, the other goes down. As previously explained, a table that shows no Chi Square, Gamma or Cramer's V information had no statistical significance and is presented only to show disparity between it and a corresponding table.

Tables 2.3–2.17—Number of Years in the Priesthood

2.3 *Honoring Vows—Believe:* All priests said they believe in the importance of honoring vows. 6.7 percent of those in the priesthood 21–30 years were noncommittal.

2.4 *Honoring Vows—Adhere:* Notice how much the percentages shifted between Tables 2.3 and 2.4 when they were asked if they adhere to their vows because of their belief in the importance of honoring vows. The longer priests remained in the priesthood, the more they said they adhere because of the importance of honoring vows. Newly ordained (0–10 years) priests who have just taken vows have the lowest percentage of *strongly agree* in this question (16.7 percent) and the highest percentage of the noncommitted (13.3 percent) were among priests in the priesthood 21–30 years (p<.001).

2.5 *Divine Retribution—Believe:* None of the priests in the priesthood 21–30 years said they believe in divine retribution (sinful) for breaking vows. Only one-third of the newly ordained agreed, none strongly agreed. In fact, the only demographic in which a majority agreed that it is sinful to break vows were respondents in the priesthood over 41 years.

2.6 *Divine Retribution—Adhere:* None of the newly ordained priests said that priests adhere to their vows because of divine retribution for breaking vows. Also, priests in the priesthood 21–30 years were either non-committal or disagreed.

2.7 *Priests Break Vows:* No one disagreed that priests break their vows, but 18.8 percent of priests in the priesthood 41+ years were noncommittal.

2.8 *Sexual Freedom in Secular Society—Believe:* Newly ordained priests agreed with the least conviction among all priests that there is sexual freedom in society. Given that the newly ordained priests experienced sexual freedom more recently than those who are viewing from the inside, it seems that the opposite would be true.

Table 2.3	Years in Priesthood/Believe Honor Vows Important				
Years in Priesthood	**SA**	**A**	**NAD**	**D**	**SD**
0–10 years	50.0%	50.0%	0.0%	0.0%	0.0%
11–20 years	82.4%	17.6%	0.0%	0.0%	0.0%
21–30 years	86.7%	6.7%	6.7%	0.0%	0.0%
31–40 years	81.0%	19.0%	0.0%	0.0%	0.0%
41+ years	93.3%	6.7%	0.0%	0.0%	0.0%

Gamma −.330; p<.121

Table 2.4	Years in Priesthood/Adhere Because of Importance of Honoring Vows				
Years in Priesthood	**SA**	**A**	**NAD**	**D**	**SD**
0–10 years	16.7%	83.3%	0.0%	0.0%	0.0%
11–20 years	35.3%	52.9%	5.9%	5.9%	0.0%
21–30 years	46.7%	40.0%	13.3%	0.0%	0.0%
31–40 years	61.9%	33.3%	4.8%	0.0%	0.0%
41+ years	81.3%	12.5%	0.0%	6.3%	0.0%

Gamma: –.451; p<.001

Table 2.5	Years in Priesthood/Believe in Divine Retribution* for Breaking Vows (*sinful)					
Years in Priesthood	**SA**	**A**	**NAD**	**D**	**SD**
0–10 years	0.0%	33.3%	16.7%	50.0%	0.0%
11–20 years	11.8%	11.8%	23.5%	29.4%	23.5%
21–30 years	0.0%	0.0%	26.7%	33.3%	40.0%
31–40 years	21.1%	21.1%	26.3%	21.1%	10.5%
41+ years	20.0%	40.0%	0.0%	40.0%	0.0%

Gamma: –.256; p<.021.

Table 2.6 Years in Priesthood/Adhere Because of Divine Retribution for Breaking Vows

Years in Priesthood	SA	A	NAD	D	SD
0–10 years	0.0%	0.0%	0.0%	33.3%	66.7%
11–20 years	5.9%	5.9%	5.9%	52.9%	29.4%
21–30 years	0.0%	0.0%	20.0%	40.0%	40.0%
31–40 years	5.0%	20.0%	30.0%	25.0%	20.0%
41+ years	7.1%	14.3%	28.6%	21.4%	28.6%

Gamma: −.336; p<.007

Table 2.7	Years in Priesthood/Priests Break Vows				
Years in Priesthood	**SA**	**A**	**NAD**	**D**	**SD**
0–10 years	33.3%	66.7%	0.0%	0.0%	0.0%
11–20 years	29.4%	64.7%	5.9%	0.0%	0.0%
21–30 years	53.3%	46.7%	0.0%	0.0%	0.0%
31–40 years	47.6%	47.6%	4.8%	0.0%	0.0%
41+ years	43.8%	37.5%	18.8%	0.0%	0.0%

Table 2.8 Years in Priesthood/Believe in Sexual Freedom in Society

Years in Priesthood	SA	A	NAD	D	SD
0–10 years	0.0%	66.7%	16.7%	16.7%	0.0%
11–20 years	37.5%	56.3%	0.0%	6.3%	0.0%
21–30 years	53.3%	46.7%	0.0%	0.0%	0.0%
31–40 years	70.0%	20.0%	5.0%	0.0%	5.0%
41+ years	47.1%	47.1%	0.0%	5.9%	0.0%

Gamma: —.285; *p<.054*

2.9 *Sexual Freedom in Society—Break:* Half the newly ordained priests as well as those in the priesthood 21–30 years were either noncommittal or disagreed that priests break their vows because of sexual freedom in secular society. So, while some priest respondents believed that there is sexual freedom in secular society, a large percentage among them was noncommittal or disagreed that this is the reason priests break vows.

2.10 *Priests Break Vows Because of Sexual Needs:* The longer a priest was in the priesthood, the stronger he believed that *priests break vows because of sexual needs.* The percentage jumped from 16.7 percent (newly ordained) to 75.0 percent (31–40 years). However, 50.0 percent of the newly ordained were noncommittal. They would not admit either way.

2.11 *Does the Church Acknowledge the Breaking of Vows?* Newly ordained priests (0–10 years) and priests in the priesthood 41+ years were the only two longevity categories that strongly agreed or agreed 100 percent that the church *acknowledges* the breaking of vows.

2.12 *Does the Church Discipline the Breaking of Vows?* Over half the priests in the priesthood 21–30 years were noncommittal when asked if the church *disciplines* the breaking of vows, 21 percent more than the total sample on this question (53.3 percent versus 32.3 percent). Note the high percentages among NAD.

2.13 *Do You Adhere?*

2.14 *Are you tempted to break your vows?*

2.15 *Has there been an occasion when you did not adhere?* These questions resulted in conflicting responses: 100 percent of the newly ordained (0–10 years) said they adhere to their vows. One-third (33.3 percent) of these, however, said there were occasions when they did not adhere. 100 percent of those in the priesthood 41+ years said they adhere, but 23.1 percent said there were occasions when they did not adhere. The longer the others were in the priesthood, the more they admitted to not adhering to their vows. *Do you adhere* is presented with *tempted to break* and *occasion when vows are broken* in order to illustrate the inconsistencies in like responses, which we interpret as internal conflicts that priests have regarding their vows.

Table 2.9 Years in Priesthood/Break Vows Because of Sexual Freedom in Secular Society

Years in Priesthood	SA	A	NAD	D	SD
0–10 years	0.0%	50.0%	25.0%	25.0%	0.0%
11–20 years	18.8%	50.0%	12.5%	18.8%	0.0%
21–30 years	0.0%	50.0%	21.4%	21.4%	7.1%
31–40 years	26.3%	47.4%	15.8%	10.5%	0.0%
41+ years	26.7%	53.3%	0.0%	20.0%	0.0%

Table 2.10 | Years in Priesthood/Priests Break Vows Because of Sexual Needs

Years in Priesthood	SA	A	NAD	D	SD
0–10 years	0.0%	16.7%	50.0%	33.3%	0.0%
11–20 Years	8.3%	25.0%	41.7%	8.3%	16.7%
21–30 Years	20.0%	26.7%	40.0%	13.3%	0.0%
31–40 Years	10.0%	65.0%	15.0%	0.0%	10.0%
41+ Years	7.1%	57.1%	21.4%	7.1%	7.1%

Gamma: −.280; p<.029

Table 2.11 Years in Priesthood/Does the Church Acknowledge Priests Breaking Vows?

Years in Priesthood	SA	A	NAD	D	SD
0–10 years	33.3%	66.7%	0.0%	0.0%	0.0%
11–20 Years	18.8%	68.8%	6.3%	6.3%	0.0%
21–30 Years	20.0%	73.3%	6.7%	0.0%	0.0%
31–40 Years	50.0%	45.0%	5.0%	0.0%	0.0%
41+ Years	42.9%	57.1%	0.0%	0.0%	0.0%

Gamma: –.302; p< .048

Table 2.12 Years in Priesthood/Church Disciplines the Breaking of Vows					
No. Years in Priesthood	**SA**	**A**	**NAD**	**D**	**SD**
0–10 years	0.0%	50.0%	33.3%	16.7%	0.0%
11–20 years	7.1%	42.9%	21.4%	21.4%	7.1%
21–30 years	13.3%	26.7%	53.3%	6.7%	0.0%
31–40 years	11.8%	64.7%	17.6%	5.9%	0.0%
41+ years	15.4%	38.5%	38.5%	7.7%	0.0%

Table 2.13	Years in Priesthood/Do You Adhere to Your Vows?	
No. Years in Priesthood	**Yes**	**No**
0–10 years	100.0%	0.0%
11–20 years	88.2%	11.8%
21–30 years	80.0%	20.0%
31–40 years	76.2%	23.8%
41+ years	100.0%	0.0%

Table 2.14 Years in Priesthood/Are You Tempted to Break Your Vows?

No. Years in Priesthood	Frequently	Occasionally	Not Often	Never
0–10 years	0.0%	66.7%	33.3%	0.0%
11–20 years	5.9%	47.1%	23.5%	23.5%
21–30 years	26.7%	40.0%	20.0%	13.3%
31–40 years	23.8%	57.1%	9.5%	9.5%
41+ years	11.8%	47.1%	29.4%	11.8%

Table 2.15 | Years in Priesthood/Has There Been an Occasion When You Did Not Adhere?

No. Years in Priesthood	Yes	No
0–10 years	33.3%	66.7%
11–20 years	38.5%	61.5%
21–30 years	42.9%	57.1%
31–40 years	63.2%	36.8%
41+ years	23.1%	76.9%

2.16 *Do you believe in optional celibacy?*

2.17 *Do you believe priests should be allowed to marry?* The strongest support for *optional celibacy* was among those in the priesthood 21–30 years: 93.3 percent versus 69.9 percent in the total sample. This was the highest response rate on the question among all demographics in cross-tabulations. In addition, it was the only longevity category that was consistent (93.3 percent) when asked if priests should be allowed to marry, essentially the same question. Table 2.17 demonstrates again the conflicting attitudes among priests in all longevity categories on similar questions. For instance, while 100 percent of priests in the priesthood 41+ years said priests should be allowed to marry, only 60 percent (40 percent fewer) said they believe in optional celibacy.

TABLES 2.18–2.25: Age Entered Seminary

2.18 *Additional Factors for Adhering to Vows:* When asked about additional factors for adhering to their vows, 100 percent of the respondents who entered the seminary at 30 years old or older said they adhere to their vows because of their *devotion to ministry,* compared to the total sample which was one-third less. 40 percent of those entering the seminary between 16 and 19 years of age indicated *faithful to their promise* was the reason, compared to 25 percent in the total sample.

2.19 *Priests Break Vows:* 100 percent of respondents who entered the seminary at the age of 20–29 as well as 30+-year-old seminarians said that *priests break their vows.* 17.6 percent of those entering seminary between the ages of 13 and 15 were noncommittal (NAD), almost three times the total population sample (6.7 percent).

2.20 *Priests Have Sexual Needs:* No one disagreed that *priests have sexual needs* except 20 percent of priests entering the seminary at 30+ years old, almost twenty times the total population sample (1.4 percent). Among the 13– to15–year-old seminarians, 16.7 percent checked NAD, four times the total population sample (4.1 percent).

Table 2.16   Years in Priesthood/Believe in Optional Celibacy

No. Years in Priesthood	Yes	No
0–10 years	60.0%	40.0%
11–20 years	76.5%	23.5%
21–30 years	93.3%	6.7%
31–40 years	60.0%	40.0%
41+ years	60.0%	40.0%

Table 2.17 | Years in Priesthood/Should Priests be Allowed to Marry?

No. Years in Priesthood	Yes	No
0–10 years	75.0%	25.0%
11–20 years	75.0%	25.0%
21–30 years	93.3%	6.7%
31–40 years	84.6%	15.4%
41+ years	100.0%	0.0%

Table 2.18	Age Entered Seminary/Additional Factors for Adhering to the Vows				
No. Years in Priesthood	Devotion to Ministry	Faithful to Promise	Reputation	Other	
13–15 years old	84.6%	15.4%	0.0%	0.0%	
16–19 years old	60.0%	40.0%	0.0%	0.0%	
20–29 years old	61.5%	15.4%	15.4%	7.7%	
30+ years old	100.0%	0.0%	0.0%	0.0%	

Chi Square: .069

Table 2.19	Age Entered Seminary/Priests Break Vows				
Age of Entry	**SA**	**A**	**NAD**	**D**	**SD**
13–15 years old	17.6%	64.7%	17.6%	0.0%	0.0%
16–19 years old	53.1%	40.6%	6.3%	0.0%	0.0%
20–29 years old	52.4%	47.6%	0.0%	0.0%	0.0%
30+ years old	20.0%	80.0%	0.0%	0.0%	0.0%

Chi Square: .077

Table 2.20   Age Entered Seminary/Priests Have Sexual Needs

Age of Entry	SA	A	NAD	D	SD
13–15 years old	27.8%	55.6%	16.7%	0.0%	0.0%
16–19 years old	48.4%	51.6%	0.0%	0.0%	0.0%
20–29 years old	36.8%	63.2%	0.0%	0.0%	0.0%
30+ years old	40.0%	40.0%	0.0%	20.0%	0.0%

Cramers V: .335; p<.004

2.21 *Priests Break Vows Because of Sexual Needs:* Though the groups of priests who entered seminary at 16–19 and 20–29 years of age agreed 100 percent that *priests have sexual needs*, as noted in Table 2.20, they said they do not believe as strongly that this is the reason that priests break their vows. Almost one-third (32.3 percent) of the 16- to 19-year-olds, and more than half (53.0 percent) among 20-to 29-year-olds were noncommittal or disagreed that priests break their vows because of sexual needs even though they all agreed that priests have sexual needs (Table 2.20).

2.22 *Additional Factors for Breaking Vows:* *Loneliness* (lack of intimacy, marriage, and family) was written in by every age of entry group. Most affected by loneliness were priests who entered the seminary between 20 and 29 (80 percent) and those who entered the seminary prior to the age of 20 (over 50 percent). Among the total population sample, the figure was 59.3 percent.

2.23 *Church Discipline—How Often:* When asked *how often* the church *disciplines* the breaking of vows, 68.8 percent of those entering the priesthood between 13 and 15 years old said *not often* or *never* compared to the total sample of 37.3 percent. *Public knowledge* was freely written in by all age-of-entry groups except those entering the seminary between the ages of 20 and 29 (0.0 percent).

2.24 *Adhere to Vow:* Among the 16- to 19-year-old seminarians, 25 percent said they do not adhere to their vows. This number is almost double the percentage of the total priest population. When the measurement is read from the standpoint of all priests who responded that they do not adhere to their vows, 16- to 19-year-old seminarians made up 80 percent of that population.

2.25 *Priests Allowed to Marry:* The younger the priest was when he entered seminary, the more he agreed that priests should be *allowed to marry*: from 100 percent among 13-to 15-year-olds to only 40.0 percent among 30+ seminarians. In the total priest sample, 86.5 percent agreed that priests should be allowed to marry.

Table 2.21	Age Entered Seminary/Priests Break Vows Because of Sexual Needs					
Age of Entry	**SA**	**A**	**NAD**	**D**	**SD**
13–15 years old	0.0%	40.0%	40.0%	6.7%	13.3%
16–19 years old	12.9%	54.8%	19.4%	3.2%	9.7%
20–29 years old	17.6%	29.4%	41.2%	11.8%	0.0%
30+ years old	0.0%	25.0%	25.0%	50.0%	0.0%

Table 2.22	Age Entered Seminary/Additional Factors for Breaking Vows						
Age of Entry	Loneliness	Weakness	Societal	Lack of Prayer	Church Issues	Substance Abuse	Other
13–15 years old	53.3%	20.0%	0.0%	6.7%	6.7%	13.3%	0.0%
16–19 years old	58.3%	20.8%	4.2%	8.3%	4.2%	4.2%	0.0%
20–29 years old	80.0%	6.7%	0.0%	6.7%	6.7%	0.0%	0.0%
30+ years old	20.0%	20.0%	0.0%	0.0%	20.0%	20.0%	20.0%

Table 2.23	Age Entered Seminary/How Often Does the Church Discipline?				
Age of Entry	**Frequently**	**Occasionally**	**Not Often**	**Never**	**Public Knowledge**
13–15 years old	0.0%	25.0%	25.0%	43.8%	6.3%
16–19 years old	20.7%	44.8%	6.9%	17.2%	10.3%
20–29 years old	5.9%	52.9%	17.6%	23.5%	0.0%
30+ years old	20.0%	60.0%	0.0%	0.0%	20.0%

Gamma: –.271; p<.038

Table 2.24 Age Entered Seminary/Do You Adhere to Your Vows?

Age of Entry	Yes	No
13–15 years old	94.4%	5.6%
16–19 years old	75.0%	25.0%
20–29 years old	95.2%	4.8%
30+ years old	100.0%	0.0%

Chi Square: .075

Table 2.25	Age Entered Seminary/Should Priests Be Allowed to Marry?	
Age of Entry	**Yes**	**No**
13–15 years old	100.0%	0.0%
16–19 years old	95.5%	4.5%
20–29 years old	76.9%	23.1%
30+ years old	40.0%	60.0%

Chi Square: .003

Tables 2.26–2.27—Type of Priest

2.26 *Divine Retribution—Belief:* 50.0 percent of religious order priests and 23 percent of diocesan priests said they *believe in divine retribution for breaking vows.* The total sample percentage was 31.9 percent. However, 56.3 percent of diocesan priests do not believe it is a sin to break their vows.

2.27 *Divine Retribution—Adhere:* Only 26 percent of religious order and 8.2 percent of diocesan priests said they *adhere because of the belief in divine retribution.* The total sample percentage was 13.9 percent.

Tables 2.28–2.32: Number of Assignments in 10 Years

2.28 *Divine Retribution—Believe:* The more assignments a priest had in 10 years, the less he said he *believes* in divine retribution (sinful) for breaking vows. In fact, none (0.0 percent) of the priest respondents who had 5–10 assignments in 10 years said they *believe in divine retribution for breaking vows.* 60.0 percent of those with 5–10 assignments in 10 years did not commit either way (NAD), which when compared to the total sample of 19.4 percent is significant. (It is common knowledge that priest offenders were frequently moved from parish to parish.)

2.29 *Divine Retribution—Adhere:* The more times a priest was relocated in 10 years, the less he said he adheres to his vows because of his belief in divine retribution for breaking vows. In fact, 100 percent of those with 5–10 assignments in ten years D or SD.

Table 2.26 Type of Priest/Believe in Divine Retribution for Breaking Vows

Age of Entry	SA	A	NAD	D	SD
Diocesan	6.3%	16.7%	20.8%	37.5%	18.8%
Religious Order	25.0%	25.0%	16.7%	20.8%	12.5%

Gamma: –.389; p <.027

Table 2.27 Type of Priest/Adhere Because of Belief in Divine Retribution

Age of Entry	SA	A	NAD	D	SD
Diocesan	0.0%	8.2%	16.3%	34.7%	40.8%
Religious Order	13.0%	13.0%	26.1%	34.8%	13.0%

Gamma: –.525; p<.002

Table 2.28 # Assignments in 10 Years/Believe in Divine Retribution for Breaking Vows

# Assignments	SA	A	NAD	D	SD
1–2 assignments	13.3%	22.2%	17.8%	37.8%	8.9%
3–4 assignments	0.0%	12.5%	18.8%	31.3%	37.5%
5–10 assignments	0.0%	0.0%	60.0%	20.0%	20.0%

Gamma: .388; p<.014

Table 2.29 # Assignments in 10 Years/Adhere Because of Belief in Divine Retribution

# Assignments	SA	A	NAD	D	SD
1–2 assignments	4.4%	13.3%	24.4%	31.1%	26.7%
3–4 assignments	0.0%	0.0%	17.6%	47.1%	35.3%
5–10 assignments	0.0%	0.0%	0.0%	40.0%	60.0%

Gamma: .447; p<.008

2.30 *Sexual Freedom in Society:* The more times a priest was relocated in 10 years, the less he said he agrees that there is sexual freedom in society (p<.001).

2.31 *Priests Break Vows Because of Sexual Needs:* The more times a priest was relocated in 10 years, the less he said he believes that priests break vows because of sexual needs. Only 20 percent of priests with 5–10 assignments in 10 years said they believe that priests break their vows because of sexual needs, which, when compared to 53.7 percent among the total sample is significant. This question also received very high NAD—56.3 percent among those with 3–4 assignments and 40.0 percent with 5–10 assignments in 10 years, compared to 29.9 percent among the total sample.

2.32 *Do You Adhere?* 40.0 percent of priests who had 5–10 assignments in 10 years admitted that they *do not adhere to their vows*, more than three times the number of the total sample (13.2 percent).

In 2004, interrelations between the dependent variables were re-examined and some significant relationships were found with the variable *Priests break vows*, as indicated in Tables 2.33–2.38.

Tables 2.33–2.38—Priests Break Vows

2.33 *Priests Break Vows/Priests Have Sexual Needs:* 63.3 percent of respondents who strongly agreed that priests break vows also strongly agreed that priests have sexual needs, compared to 39.7 percent of the total sample who responded SA that priests have sexual needs. 25 percent of the respondents who were noncommittal about priests breaking vows were also noncommittal about priests having sexual needs, which when compared to the total sample of respondents of 4.1 percent is significant (p<.001).

2.34 *Priests Break Vows/Priests Break Their Vows Because of Sexual Needs:* Two-thirds of the respondents who were noncommittal about priests breaking their vows SD that they do so because of sexual needs. Notice the double digit percentages in the NAD column (p<.001).

Table 2.30 # Assignments in 10 Years/Believe in Sexual Freedom in Secular Society

# Assignments	SA	A	NAD	D	SD
1–2 assignments	59.6%	40.4%	0.0%	0.0%	0.0%
3–4 assignments	35.3%	52.9%	0.0%	11.8%	0.0%
5–10 assignments	20.0%	40.0%	20.0%	20.0%	0.0%

Cramers V: .406; p>.001

Table 2.31 # Assignments in 10 Years/Priests Break Vows Because of Sexual Needs

# Assignments	SA	A	NAD	D	SD
1–2 assignments	9.8%	56.1%	19.5%	9.8%	4.9%
3–4 assignments	12.5%	18.8%	56.3%	6.3%	6.3%
5–10 assignments	20.0%	0.0%	40.0%	20.0%	20.0%

Gamma: .344; p<.071

Table 2.32   # Assignments in 10 years/Do You Adhere to Your Vows?

# Assignments	Yes	No
1–2 assignments	85.4%	14.6%
3–4 assignments	100.0%	0.0%
5–10 assignments	60.0%	40.0%

Chi Square: .052

Table 2.33 Priests Break Vows/Priests Have Sexual Needs

	SA	A	NAD	D	SD
SA	63.3%	33.3%	3.3%	0.0%	0.0%
A	23.7%	71.1%	2.6%	2.6%	0.0%
NAD	25.0%	50.0%	25.0%	0.0%	0.0%

Gamma: .600; p<.001

Table 2.34 Priests Break Vows/Priests Break Vows Because of Sexual Needs

	SA	A	NAD	D	SD
SA	24.1%	34.5%	31.0%	6.9%	3.4%
A	0.0%	55.9%	29.4%	8.8%	5.9%
NAD	0.0%	0.0%	33.3%	0.0%	66.7%

Cramers V: .638; p<.001

2.35 *Priests Break Vows/Church Acknowledges:* Nearly all (94.3 percent) who admitted that priests break vows said the Church acknowledges that priests break vows. 71.9 percent strongly agreed, compared to the total sample, of which only 33.8 percent strongly agreed (p<.0001).

2.36 *Priests Break Vows/Church Disciplines:* Almost half of the respondents who SA that priests break vows were noncommittal about whether or not the church disciplines the breaking of vows, compared to the total sample of 32.3 percent who were noncommittal.

2.37 *Priests Break Vows/How Often Does the Church Discipline?* All (100 percent) of the respondents who were noncommittal about priests breaking vows said that discipline takes place only when there is public knowledge. As previously indicated public knowledge was a write-in response; it was not listed as an option on the survey instrument (p<.0001).

2.38 *Priests Break Vows Because of Sexual Needs/Additional Factors—Adhere:* 75 percent of priests who break vows because of sexual needs responded that priests adhere to their vows because they are faithful to their promise. Since the percentage was so high, this data makes us question whether the breaking of vows in many instances may be something some priests simply cannot control.

Table 2.39—Church Response

In view of the fact that church response, or lack thereof, to clergy sex abuse has become a major issue since January 2002 (one of the reasons Boston's Cardinal Law stepped down), the church discipline questions were reexamined in 2004 and measured against one another, producing a significant intercorrelation not previously seen.

2.39 *Church Discipline/How Often Church Disciplines:* All of the respondents who were noncommittal about whether or not the church *disciplines* the breaking of vows said that the discipline takes place *only when there is public knowledge.* It would seem they did not want to admit it (p<.001).

Table 2.35	Priests Break Vows/Church Acknowledges the Breaking of Vows				
	SA	**A**	**NAD**	**D**	**SD**
SA	71.9%	28.1%	0.0%	0.0%	0.0%
A	2.6%	86.8%	7.9%	2.6%	0.0%
NAD	0.0%	0.0%	0.0%	0.0%	0.0%
D	0.0%	0.0%	0.0%	0.0%	0.0%
SD	0.0%	0.0%	0.0%	0.0%	0.0%

Gamma: .980; p<.0001

Table 2.36 Priests Break Vows/Church Disciplines the Breaking of Vows

	SA	A	NAD	D	SD
SA	20.0%	23.3%	46.7%	10.0%	0.0%
A	2.9%	62.9%	20.0%	11.4%	2.9%
NAD	0.0%	0.0%	0.0%	0.0%	0.0%
D	0.0%	0.0%	0.0%	0.0%	0.0%
SD	0.0%	0.0%	0.0%	0.0%	0.0%

Cramers V: .472; p<.006

Table 2.37 Priests Break Vows/How Often Does the Church Discipline?

Priests Break Vows	Frequently	Occasionally	Not Often	Never	Public Knowledge*
SA	22.7%	50.0%	22.7%	0.0%	4.5%
A	11.1%	66.7%	14.8%	3.7%	3.7%
NAD	0.0%	0.0%	0.0%	0.0%	100.0%

Chi Square: p:<.0001
Very significant because of write-in response

Table 2.38 Priests Break Vows because of Sexual Needs/Additional Factors for Adhering to Vows

	SA	A	NAD	D	SD
Devotion to Ministry	0.0%	47.1%	35.3%	11.8%	5.9%
Faithful to Promise	41.7%	33.3%	16.7%	8.3%	0.0%
Reputation	100.0%	0.0%	0.0%	0.0%	0.0%
Other	0.0%	0.0%	100.0%	0.0%	0.0%

Gamma: −.559; p<.012

Table 2.39 | Church Disciplines the Breaking of Vows/How Often Does the Church Discipline?

How Often?	SA	A	NAD	D	SD
Frequently	62.5%	37.5%	0.0%	0.0%	0.0%
Occasionally	7.4%	66.7%	22.2%	3.7%	0.0%
Not Often	0.0%	33.3%	33.3%	33.3%	0.0%
Never	0.0%	100.0%	0.0%	0.0%	0.0%
*Public Knowledge	0.0%	0.0%	100.0%	0.0%	0.0%

*Chi Square: p:<.001 *Write in response*

2.40–2.43—Demographic Relationships (Intervening Variables):

Tables 2.40–2.43 examine more closely, the demographics of our respondents (i.e., how many respondents who were in the priesthood 21–30 years had entered seminary between 13–15 years old?).

2.40 *Number of Years in the Priesthood/Age of Entry into Seminary:* There is a significant drop in number of years in the priesthood among those who entered seminary between the ages of 13 and 15 years old and of 20 and 29 years old. We would suggest that this is indicative of priests who had left to marry rather than policy changes in recruitment.

2.41 *Number of Years in the Priesthood/Type of Priest:* Table 2.41 illustrates the length of service that the two types of priests have given to the church. We anticipated very different responses from priests living in closed communities as opposed to those living in parish houses. Our data indicate that the internal conflict that exists among priests may have nothing to do with their housing environment.

2.42. *Number of Years in the Priesthood/Number of Assignments in 10 Years*

2.43 *Age Entered Seminary/Number of Assignments in 10 Years* We believe that Tables 2.42 and 2.43 are important because one of the legal issues regarding clergy sexual abuse relates to the number of times a bishop moved a priest from parish to parish, or in some cases, from diocese to diocese, the latter of which implicates more than one bishop in aiding and abetting sexual abuse. In the case of Age of Entry, it appears that there are risks no matter what age the seminarian is when he enters, contrary to the current belief that an older seminarian is a "safer" seminarian.

Table 2.40 Number of Years in the Priesthood/Age Entered Seminary

No. of Years	13–15 Years old	16–19 Years Old	20–29 Years Old	30+ Years Old
0–10 Years	0.0%	16.7%	50.0%	33.3%
11–20 Years	29.4%	23.5%	41.2%	5.9%
21–30 Years	20.0%	60.0%	6.7%	13.3%
31–40 Years	19.0%	57.1%	23.8%	0.0%
41+ Years	35.3%	35.3%	29.4%	0.0%

Gamma: –.247; p:<.047

Table 2.41   Number of Years in the Priesthood/Type of Priest

No. Years in Priesthood	Diocesan	Religious Order
0–10 Years	100.0%	0.0%
11–20 Years	76.5%	23.5%
21–30 Years	80.0%	20.0%
31–40 Years	47.6%	52.4%
41+ Years	58.8%	41.2%

Table 2.42	Number of Years in the Priesthood/# of Assignments in 10 Years		
No. Years	1–2 Assignments	3–4 Assignments	5–10 Assignments
0–10 years	50.0%	33.3%	16.7%
11–20 years	43.8%	43.8%	12.5%
21–30 years	66.7%	20.0%	13.3%
31–40 years	84.2%	15.8%	0.0%
41+ years	68.6%	24.3%	7.1%

Gamma: −.501; p< .001

Table 2.43 Age Entered Seminary/# of Assignments in 10 Years

# Assignments	13–15 years old	16–19 years old	20–29 years old	30+ years old
1–2 assignments	25.0%	47.9%	18.8%	8.3%
3–4 assignments	23.5%	29.4%	47.1%	0.0%
5–10 assignments	20.0%	40.0%	20.0%	20.0%

Gamma: –.415; p<.160

Comments from Priest Respondents [sic]

General Comments:

"I was a Diocesan priest for 20 years. A diocesan priest makes a solemn promise of celibacy, not a vow. Nearly 2 years ago I became a religious priest and took the vow of celibacy. It is much easier for me to adhere to the structure of religious community than when isolated from other priests in a diocesan situation. It is important for diocesan priests to have a support structure of other priests and other people who are supportive of his living a pure celibate life. For some people to be living a celibate life carries a strong sign value for people living in a very promiscuous society."

....

"I appreciate what you are trying to do with this survey. However, popular opinion has little influence on the Roman Catholic Church. See what happened to the women's ordination issue. There is hope in the future because the church has a 1000 year old tradition of a married clergy; from the time of Christ to the 11th century, priests were married."

....

"A person studying for the priesthood in a seminary or monastery has 8–10 years to prepare himself. Knowing what the vow of celibacy requires of him, you may go ahead taking the vow and later then say priests should be allowed to marry. They know that before they took the vow. A person married cannot give himself completely to God. He is divided between wife, family, and God."

....

"As a young priest I had great difficulty with celibacy both in theory and in practice. In 1994 in treatment for depression, I learned that

I did not recognize how grief was involved in the 1960's when many priest friends left the priesthood—and how that made me very rebellious against the vow of celibacy. Now, at age 61, I am more inclined to accept life as it is, and now am very determined to live a chaste priestly life despite past failures, which I have also learned to live with and accept as where I was that time."

"Chastity is not the same as celibacy. I promised "celibacy," not chastity. Chastity is + or - a Christian approach to sex."

"Unfortunately some of our priests have broken their vows of celibacy or chastity out of a sense of loneliness, as well as through addictions. Many do not experience dating before they go into the seminary which causes them to work out what they had missed by not dating.

"The whole question of sexuality desires needs to be reviewed and studied. I am not sure that there should be total freedom—nor am I sure that there should be total denial. The newspapers tell us that often the reality is different than the ideals striven for. I find it unfortunate that this is the only question you focus on. The questions have different answers for celibacy than they do for chastity. They are not the same. I have answered referring only to chastity.

Question 13 (additional factors for adhering to the vows):

"They see it as God's call for them to be best able to serve their spouse, the church."

"Celibacy is a gift from God and frees you to be with your community of faith."

"Preference for freedom and flexibility of the single lifestyle—mobility to deal with some dimensions & long-term interpersonal relationships."

"Dedication to their priesthood and ministry to God and his people."

....

"I believe we should be faithful to a promise."

....

"Yes, love for the church; and I believe many priests see celibacy/chastity as a powerful enhancement to fruitful ministry."

....

"The majority of priests adhere to celibacy, primarily because of their love for Christ and the church. Retribution has no sense in this matter."

....

"Love for Christ and the church. Accepting celibacy as a viable and happy way to love and serve."

....

"Yes because the discipline of the church requires celibacy at this time—no other reason for Diocesan priests."

....

"Prayer—regularly and often."

Question 23 (Other factors for breaking vows):

"Finding out after their vow has been made that God seems to be calling them to the marriage state. Giving in to sexual temptation."

....

"Loneliness, a need to be loved; a need to give the totality of their being in a relationship."

....

"Loneliness, need for support + affirmation longing for more 'human connectedness.'"

....

"Loneliness, need for intimacy for more important cause than 'sexual needs' in majority of cases."

....

"Loneliness; desire to 'feel close' to someone else."

....

"Psychological factors such as inability to fulfill needs for intimacy and love within comfort of vows. Loneliness can become overpowering. Human weakness and tendency to yield to temptation also a big factor. Also, many priests believe it is unfair to link priesthood and celibacy as a mandatory requirement for priestly ministry."

"Alcohol can often lessen one's inhibitions and thereby be a factor where total sobriety would have avoided this occasion."

"They are missing something very important: the spirituality of a person. A priest without spirituality is better off quitting the priesthood."

"This is a complex issue! Need is one factor, but I also believe that love is another factor which is much more important to consider. Relationship is another factor."

"Because some may suddenly realize (probably after ordination) that they are not naturally gifted with the virtue of chastity, even though they have the gift of ordination."

"Being subject to occupational pressures and stress. Getting emotionally and inordinately involved with dependent parishioners."

"Frustration, loneliness."

"It's always a mixed bag. Rarely one factors loneliness, discouragement, lack of respect/results in work, falls in love, stops praying + committing himself to God. Psych. factors; bombardment of a sexual culture."

"A priest can become lonely, feel unappreciated and lose the spiritual motivation, or the complexity of human relationships is always challenging between men and women, vowed in marriage or celibacy. A lifetime of fidelity is more a question of continuity of heart rather than score-keeping."

"Loneliness; weak appropriate relationship supported groups + my God: intimacy need is not upheld in a good way."

....

"Stress, frustration, nit-picky, unhealthy lifestyle (living at the office), lack of personal life and friends, overwork, etc."

(Haggett, Hanson and Solo 1997)

Survey Instrument

(Haggett, Hanson and Solo, 1997)

General Instructions: Please place a checkmark on the line beside your choice of answer, or write in an answer where necessary.

The following questions are to establish general information about our respondents.

1. How many years have you been a priest?
2. At what age did you enter the seminary?
3. Did you date prior to becoming ordained?
   (Please check one)
   a. Frequently
   b. Occasionally
   c. Not Often
   d. Never

4. What type of priest are you?
   a. Diocesan
   b. Religious Order

5. How long have you been at your present assignment?

6. How many assignments have you had in the past ten years?

(Continued on next page)

The following questions are about your attitudes regarding priests and the church. For most of these questions, you will be asked to indicate your agreement or disagreement with a statement.

7. I believe in priestly divinity.
   (Please check one)
   a. Strongly agree
   b. Agree
   c. Neither agree nor disagree
   d. Disagree
   e. Strongly disagree

8. I believe that priests adhere to the vow of celibacy/chastity because of a belief in priestly divinity.
   (Please check one)
   a. Strongly agree
   b. Agree
   c. Neither agree nor disagree
   d. Disagree
   e. Strongly disagree

9. I believe that honoring a vow is important.
   (Please check one)
   a. Strongly agree
   b. Agree
   c. Neither agree nor disagree
   d. Disagree
   e. Strongly disagree

10. I believe that priests who adhere to the vow of celibacy/chastity do so because they believe in the importance of honoring vows.
    (Please check one)
    a. Strongly agree
    b. Agree
    c. Neither agree nor disagree
    d. Disagree
    e. Strongly disagree

11. I believe in divine retribution for breaking vows.
    (Please check one)

    a. Strongly agree
    b. Agree
    c. Neither agree nor disagree
    d. Disagree
    e. Strongly disagree

12. I believe that priests who adhere to the vow of celibacy/chastity do so because of a belief in divine retribution.
    (Please check one)

    a. Strongly agree
    b. Agree
    c. Neither agree nor disagree
    d. Disagree
    e. Strongly disagree

13. Are there any additional factors that you feel contribute to priests adhering to their vow of celibacy/chastity?

    _____
    _____
    _____
    _____
    _____
    _____
    _____

14. I believe that priests break their vow of celibacy/chastity.
    (Please check one)

    a. Strongly agree   *Please go to question 15*
    b. Agree   *Please go to question 15*
    c. Neither agree nor disagree   *Please go to question 18*
    d. Disagree   *Please go to question 18*
    e. Strongly disagree   *Please go to question 18*

(Continued on next page)

15. I believe that the church acknowledges that some priests break the vow of celibacy/chastity.
    (Please check one)

    a. Strongly agree   *Please go to question 16*
    b. Agree   *Please go to question 16*
    c. Neither agree nor disagree   *Please go to question 18*
    d. Disagree   *Please go to question 18*
    e. Strongly disagree   *Please go to question 18*

16. I believe that the church disciplines priests who break the vow of celibacy/chastity.
    (Please check one)

    a. Strongly agree   *Please go to question 17*
    b. Agree   *Please go to question 17*
    c. Neither agree nor disagree   *Please go to question 18*
    d. Disagree   *Please go to question 18*
    e. Strongly disagree   *Please go to question 18*

17. How often do you believe the church disciplines priests who break their vow of celibacy/chastity?
    (Please check one)

    Frequently
    Occasionally
    Not often
    Never

18. I believe that there is sexual freedom in secular society.
    (Please check one)

    a. Strongly agree   *Please go to question 19*
    b. Agree   *Please go to question 19*
    c. Neither agree nor disagree   *Please go to question 20*
    d. Disagree   *Please go to question 20*
    e. Strongly disagree   *Please go to question 20*

19. I believe that priests who break the vow of celibacy/chastity are influenced in their behavior by sexual freedom in secular society.
(Please check one)

a. Strongly agree
b. Agree
c. Neither agree nor disagree
d. Disagree
e. Strongly disagree

20. I believe that people in secular society have natural sexual needs.
(Please check one)

a. Strongly agree
b. Agree
c. Neither agree nor disagree
d. Disagree
e. Strongly disagree

21. I believe that priests have natural sexual needs.
(Please check one)

a. Strongly agree   *Please go to question 22*
b. Agree   *Please go to question 22*
c. Neither agree nor disagree   *Please go to question 22*
d. Disagree   *Please go to question 22*
e. Strongly disagree   *Please go to question 22*

22. I believe that priests who break the vow of celibacy/chastity do so because of sexual needs.
(Please check one)

a. Strongly agree
b. Agree
c. Neither agree nor disagree
d. Disagree
e. Strongly disagree

(Continued on next page)

23. Are there any additional factors that you feel contribute to priests breaking their vow of celibacy/chastity?

_____

_____

_____

24. Do you adhere to your vow of celibacy/chastity?
    a. Yes
    b. No

25. Have you ever been tempted to break your vow of celibacy/chastity?
    (Please check one)

    a. Frequently   *Please go to question 26*
    b. Occasionally   *Please go to question 26*
    c. Not often   *Please go to question 26*
    d. Never   *Please go to question 27*

26. Has there ever been an occasion when you did not adhere to your vow of celibacy/chastity?
    a. Yes
    b. No

27. Do you believe in optional celibacy?
    a. Yes   *Please go to question 28*
    b. No   *Please go to end of survey*

28. Do you believe that priests should be allowed to marry?
    a. Yes
    b. No

We are interested in any other comments you might have regarding celibacy/chastity among priests.

This completes the survey. Thank you for your time and cooperation.

3

A Study of Victims in
Three Sections (1999)

The Victim Study was conducted by the Center for the Study of Religious Issues (CSRI). Its purpose was to investigate whether or not clergy sexual abuse was like child sexual abuse among the general population or whether there were differences. In order to make the analysis, our findings were compared to a compilation of 19 general population studies of child sexual abuse (Finkelhor 1994), chosen for its comprehensive summarization and the fact that these were adult retrospective studies—adults talking about their childhood experiences—similar to our own target population. When we discovered that over 30% of the CSRI respondents were adult victims, however, it became necessary to create separate reports so that analogous comparisons could be made. The Victim Study, therefore, is reported in three sections.

The first section (chapter 3) involves data comparisons between our findings and those from the 19-study summarization of child sexual abuse among the general population (Finkelhor ibid.). This section was peer-reviewed and accepted for and presented at national annual conferences of the Society for the Scientific Study of Religion

(Boston, December 1999) and the Eastern Sociological Society (Baltimore, March 2000).

The Adult Victim Study (chapter 4) is presented here for the first time and provides survey results of adult victims of Roman Catholic clergy.

Chapter 5, also published here for the first time, discusses findings regarding when the abuse was reported as well as, from a victim's perspective, what the possible needs of the priest(s) were.

Our findings indicate a different demographic pattern and profile among both perpetrator and child victims, thus *disproving that child sexual abuse by Roman Catholic clergy is similar to general population abuse*. This is an original study.

The tables presented in the Victim Study are included within the framework of the respective chapters to show comparative data between these and general population statistics.

Is a Sexually Abusing Roman Catholic Priest a Pedophile?
The Case for Ephebophilia

November 7, 1999; updated 2004

The Center for the Study of Religious Issues wishes to express its deep gratitude to the late Fr. Tom Economus and the members of Linkup, a national support organization for victim/survivors of sexual abuse, for their cooperation and assistance regarding this study. Fr. Economus was national coordinator of Linkup until his death in March, 2002. Thanks especially to Professor Lucille Lawless of Framingham State College, without whose mentoring neither this study nor the report would have been possible.

General Problem

Researchers and victim reporting agencies agree sexual abuse occurs so frequently that it constitutes a public health problem (Abel and Rouleau 1995). Unfortunately, the largest concentration of victims falls into the category of innocent children, causing severe injury and impairment depending on the type of abuse, according to the National Incidence Study of Child Abuse and Neglect (NIS) from a study that was supported by the Office for Victims of Crime, U.S. Department of Justice (Sedlak 1991). The NIS Study reported a prevalence of 500,000 child sexual abuse victims per year under the age of 18 in this country alone.[1] The American Psychiatric Association (APA) also confirms that children account for the largest percentage of sexual abuse victims (Zonana et al. 1998). According to APA, sexual abuse (20.2 percent) is second only to drug trafficking (37.1 percent) in prevalence as a category of violent crime. Of course, some of this increase may have to do with the freedom that more people have about reporting such violations.

While there is corroboration regarding the enormity of the crime of sexual abuse, researchers have had a difficult time analyzing the phenomenon because the terminology and methodology used in abuse studies have been too diversified to compare findings.

A 1994 summary of 19 prior sociological studies illustrates some of the confusion in child sexual abuse terminology by the following example: the target population in five of the studies ended at the age of 16; in two studies, at 17; and in ten studies, at the age of 18. Two studies simply said "during childhood" (Finkelhor 496). These methodological variations produced broad and confusing results:

- A six-year gap in peak age of victims that spans the crucial period between prepuberty and postpuberty.
- A 20-point gap regarding whether or not the perpetrator is known to the child (some researchers indicated that 70 percent of the perpetrators were known to the children, others said 90 percent).

---

[1] A January 2004 paper by Finkelhor and Jones reported a 33 percent national decline in child sexual abuse. It indicated, however, that Child Protection Services changed their method of reporting since 1993, eliminating from their statistics all cases where the perpetrator was not a family member—in other words, accepting only abuse cases that involved incest. The time frame reported in the Finkelhor et al. study also ended in the year 2000. Sexual abuse by Roman Catholic clergy did not become a widely publicized issue until January 2002. The Finkelhor et al. study also did not cite any statistics from the National Incidence Bureau, which in a prior Finkelhor report was said to be the most reliable source of information in this area (Finkelhor and Jones 2004) (Finkelhor 1994).

- A 17-percent difference in research statistics regarding whether or not child sexual abuse was primarily incestual.

Researchers have called abusers "perpetrators," "predators," "sexual offenders," "child molesters," or the term most commonly used, "pedophile," or just simply "child sexual abuse." Finkelhor (1994, Finkelhor et al. 1990) and others (Kercher and McShane 1984, Zonana et al. 1998) have recommended that uniform procedures, definitions, and terminology be applied to the issue of child sexual abuse to avoid confusion among the research community.

The most commonly-accepted definition of the most commonly-used term "pedophilia" is that which appears in APA's *Diagnostic and Statistical Manual of Mental Disorders (DSM-IV-TR)*, considered the "bible" in the mental health industry. It reads:

Pedophilia involves sexual activity by an adult with a child generally 13 years of age or younger. Some individuals prefer males, others females, and some are aroused by both males and females. Those attracted to females usually prefer 8- to 10-year-olds, whereas those attracted to males prefer slightly older children. Some pedophiles are sexually attracted only to children, whereas others are sometimes attracted to adult victims. (APA 2000:571)

The problem with this definition is that, according to APA, all perpetrators in child sexual abuse cases are considered "pedophiles," even though the victim may be a postpubescent teenager (age 13 or higher) or even an adult and these are major distinctions. While DSM-IV-TR lumps both postpubescents and adult victims in the definition of "pedophilia," the same manual provides two separate references for professional treatment of the same two groups:

- V61.21 Sexual Abuse of a Child—This category should be used when the focus of clinical attention is sexual abuse of the child.
- V62.83 Sexual Abuse of an Adult (if by person other than partner)—This category should be used when the focus of clinical attention is sexual abuse of an adult (e.g., sexual coercion, rape) (APA 2000:738).

In a special task force report in 1998, APA said that pedophiles tend to

- Cross over between touching and non touching their victims
- Cross over between family and non family members
- Cross over between female and male victims
- Crossover to victims of various ages (Zonana et al. 34)

The 1998 report also indicated "vagueness" in the term "sexual predator," particularly as it relates to "mental abnormality," in the qualification of criminal acts (Zonana et al. 1998:113). Yet, the APA's own definition of "pedophilia" as a mental disorder is just as vague.

Another complication is the target population. Some researchers call for bigger samples because of large gaps in findings, which they say make it difficult to target potential perpetrators. It's possible, however, that the solution may lie in studying subgroups of the population instead of larger general population samples.

At least three studies have concluded that delineating subgroups of the pedophile disorder may provide new information regarding aspects of the problem of child sexual abuse. Each has recommended that victim age be a criterion.

The first study (Greenberg, Bradford and Curry 1995) suggested a subcategory called "infantophilia" to accommodate the psychological differences among predators of infants to 5-year-olds. Significant differences were found between infantophiles and pedophiles in such categories as age of perpetrator and age of youngest victim. Further research would be indicated. One finding of note yielded from the Greenberg study was an overall low prior adult sexual experience (91.7 percent) among both categories of perpetrators.

The second study (Kalichman 1991) indicated that the perpetrators of adolescents were "developmentally congruent with the victims," with "some linear relationship between victim age and psychological disturbance in sexual offenders," particularly in regard to self-esteem and other social inadequacies (192).

A third study agreed that "the major difficulty in conducting or interpreting research on child sexual abuse lies in the definitions 'pedophilia' has received" (Ames and Houston 1990). They argued that a distinction should be made between biological children and sociolegal children (development versus age): "'True' pedophiles (i.e., sexually attracted to biologically prepubescent children) should not be confused with distinct types of offenders, child molesters and rapists, thereby confounding attempts to understand pedophilia" (338). The reasoning was based on their findings regarding perpetrator profiles: weak, passive, socially isolated, inept, introverted, shy, and so forth. These were descriptions of a *pedophile* in comparison with antisocial, sociopathic, defensive, and aggressive as descriptions of *adult perpetrators*. Ames and Houston believe that the broader descriptions tend to "cloud natural distinctions between child molestation and rape, hence protecting the criminal" (341). The mental health of the perpetrator is not generally considered as a defense in charges of rape, whereas it could be considered in cases of pedophilia.

Specific Problem

The CSRI hypothesis is simple: that the subgroup of priest perpetrators differs in characteristics from the general population of child sexual perpetrators. The little research that was done prior to this study where Roman Catholic clergy perpetrators were segregated from general population perpetrators indicated some distinct differences between the two groups in areas of age of perpetrator and age of victim, similar differences as those in the infantophilia study (Greenberg et al. ibid.).

The purpose of the CSRI Child and Adolescent Study is threefold:

1. To investigate possible differences between clergy sexual abuse and general population abuse
2. To further illustrate the need for segregated study populations within the categories of perpetrators
3. To add a voice to the list of those who promote more distinct and uniform terminology in describing sexual perpetrators, especially for study purposes.

Since the late 1980s, the general public has become aware of child sexual abuse cases involving Roman Catholic clergy. According to Linkup, a national support agency for clergy victims, every diocese in the United States has been implicated, a fact made public after January 2002.

Priests are an interesting study population because they allegedly live a <u>forced</u> celibate—meaning not married—lifestyle; also, they have been in a position of trust, many with access to children on a day-to-day basis. While the aggregate may be small, many perpetrators could constitute a significant and/or identifiable percentage of the non-parental sexual perpetrator population said to be 49 percent, according to NIS.

Methodology

The CSRI study population was the membership mailing list of Linkup, a national support organization for clergy abuse survivors. A self-administered questionnaire was mailed via Linkup to its confidential list of 1,199 members, comprising 959 reported victims of various sexual abuses and 240 others (parents and other supporters and professionals such as psychologists, attorneys, and prosecutors). This was an adult retrospective study of child sexual abuse, about which Finkelhor (1994) wrote, "the true scope of the problem is better reflected in retrospective surveys of adults. Adult retrospective studies are also good sources of information about the characteristics of abuse" (31). According to Finkelhor's 19-study compilation, "Many researchers have concluded that the best picture of the scope of the problem is obtained by asking adults about their childhood experiences" (34).

The CSRI study had varied questions for the victims, including some regarding their impression of the perpetrator. The basic demographic questions regarding incidence of clergy sexual abuse were compared to prevalence information from the 19-study summary (Finkelhor 1994). According to Finkelhor, prevalence figures are more realistic because of a large discrepancy between prevalence and incidence factors. With regard to the general population, Finkelhor indicated that "Less than one-third of all occurring cases are currently being identified and substantiated" (34). If this is the case with clergy sexual abuse, it could mean heavily underreported clergy abuse numbers—a much higher prevalence rate than the six percent estimate in a prior study on clergy sexual abuse (Lynch et al. 2002).

The CSRI survey was directed to *only* victims of Roman Catholic clergy abuse. Others (those who were not abused by Roman Catholic clergy or not abused at all) were asked to return the questionnaire in the self-addressed envelope provided, and were excluded from the statistics. These included surveys filled out by respondents on behalf of victims like mothers reporting abuse of multiple children, or a district attorney reporting on 16 cases. The reason for omitting these responses was to maintain survey integrity. We had no way of knowing whether the individual victims may also be on the mailing list, meaning that two reports might appear for the same individual. Hence, the valid response rate was 14% or N=131.

These responses represented 43.5% male and 56.5% female, from 76 different Catholic dioceses. Specific demographics are shown in Table 3.1.

Table 3.1	Demographics
Gender	43.5% male
	56.5% female
Geographic	76 Catholic dioceses
Age	75.6% under 55 years old at the time of the retrospective study
Education	60.0% some college
	33.1% graduate degrees
Job functions	19.7% business-related careers
	17.1% social work
	12.8% academia
	10.3% medical field
	10.3% creative arts
	10.3% disabled
	7.7% self-employed
	6.8% retired
	3.4% ministry
	1.7% blue-collar jobs

The respondents were asked how often they attended a Catholic church as a child versus their attendance today. Of the 80 percent who said they attended church 1–3 times per week as a child, 65.4 percent said they "never or hardly ever" attend today. Of those who still attend, 10.0 percent do so 1–3 times per month and 14.6 percent, 1–3 times per week. (*See next page.*)

Catholic Church Attendance as A Child

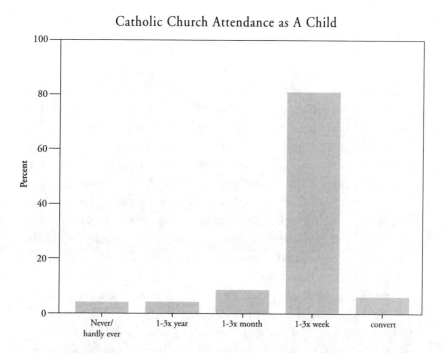

Catholic Church Attendance Today

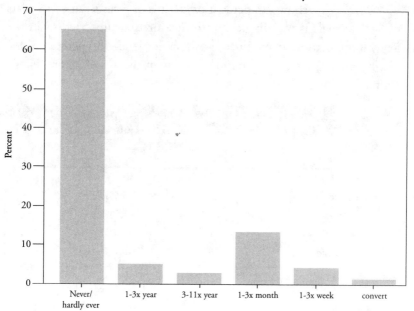

Results

As previously mentioned, this researcher's hypothesis was not specific as to what the differences are between child sexual abuse among priest offenders versus the general population—only that there is a difference between these perpetrators and general population perpetrators. Like the 1994 HIV/AIDS study published in the *Kansas City Star*, which indicated that HIV/AIDS is four times more prevalent among Roman Catholic priests than the general population (Thomas 1994), measurements in this study are irrelevant unless they are compared to general population studies. The following tables, therefore, provide more meaningful statistics because of their comparisons to prior general research. To show these percentages by themselves would do nothing to convince the scientific community of the need for targeted studies among various subgroups.

For instance, a table that shows that the peak age for incidence among clergy child and adolescent victims is 10–15 years old is insignificant until the disparity with the general public of 7–13 years old is pointed out—especially because the higher numbers for clergy victims fall into the postpubescent category of 12–14 among males (Finkelhor, 1994).

A table that shows 93 percent of victims of priests under 18 years of age are male is meaningless until measured against victims in the general population where the opposite holds true—80 percent of the victims among the general population under the age of 18 are female (Finkelhor ibid.).

Table 3.2 CSRI Incidence: Adolescent Victims of Priests		
Age	Gender	
	Male	Female
0–6 years old	0.0%	19.1%
7–9 years old	9.4%	25.5%
10–13 years old	50.9%	25.5%
14–15 years old	32.1%	10.6%
16–18 years old	7.5%	19.1%

Peak age: Clergy victims, 10–15 years old   General population*: 7–13 years old
Under 18 years old, 93% **male**   Under 18 years old, 80% **female**

Chi Square: .0001   *Finkelhor 1994—19 studies

The 19-studies summary indicated that the majority of child sexual abuse occurs between the ages of 7 and 13, representing 35 percent of all abuse (1994:48). By comparison, the CSRI retrospective survey among children and adolescents revealed that the majority of child sexual abuse victims of priests are in the 10– to 15-year-old range. Because priests' victims are older, it is also possible that the 39% figure among the 10-13 age group may be on the high end toward 13 years old, indicating postpubescent rather than prepubescent victims.

The 19-study summary said that prevalence of child sexual abuse is 80 percent female. Among priests' victims, the incidence factor is 60.3 percent male versus 51.0 percent female in the 7–13 age group; and 83 percent male and 36.1 percent female in the 10–15 age group. The CSRI study revealed an additional 36.5 percent in the female victim category among women over the age of 18, covered in chapter 4. These findings produced a chi square of .0001, indicating one chance in 10,000 that these results could be merely by chance.

A table which measures that 99.9 percent of priest perpetrators were previously known to the child is insignificant until one realizes that in the general population, a lesser figure of 70–90 percent of the perpetrators was previously known to the child.

Table 3.3 Perpetrator known to the child
99.9% of clergy perpetrators known to the child

General population*: 70–90% known to child
*Finkelhor 1994—19 studies

With regard to the duration of abuse, that 54.4 percent of child sexual abuse by priests lasts 1 year or longer is meaningless until measured against the general population. It is the incest (intrafamily) abuse that lasts 1 year or longer among the general population. In fact, 68.5 percent of child sexual abuse among the general population occurs *one time only*. By comparison, the one-time-only incidence among priest perpetrators is 19.2 percent.

Tables 3.4 and 3.5 present a possible correlation between *duration of abuse* and *form of abuse* among victims of priests. According to Finkelhor, "Acts of penetration tend to be more common among postpubescent victims in [sexual] abusive relationships that have continued over an extended period of time" (42). While the word "intercourse" or "penetration" was not used in the CSRI study, the fact that both the majority of victims are postpubescent and the duration of sexual abuse is *significantly* longer than the victims among the general population brings into question whether or not there is more penetration in clergy sexual abuse than in child sexual abuse among the general population.

Table 3.4   Duration of Abuse

Age	Gender	
	Male	Female
I time only	20.8%	13.6%
I month or less	7.5%	2.3%
I–6 months	17.0%	2.3%
6 months–I year	9.4%	11.4%
More than I year	45.3%	70.4%

Duration: Clergy victims, 17.5% I time only;
         56.7% I year or longer

General population*: 68.5% I time only

Gamma: .399; p<.002

*Finkelhor 1994—19 studies

Table 3.5   Form of Abuse

99% includes breakdown of:	
Some physical contact	1.0%
Primarily physical contact	24.0%
Physical and nonphysical**	74.0%

General population*: 20–25% female episodes involving penetration or oral-genital contact

**For this report, "nonphysical" abuse is interpreted as sexual harassment, more traumatic when it comes from someone thought to have moral authority, according to Finkelhor.

Chi Square: .0001

*Finkelhor 1994–19 studies

Table 3.6 shows that, according to this study, 47.2 percent of clergy perpetrators of children 18 and under are over 40 years old. General population figures place the average age of perpetrators in their early 30s, with one-third of the perpetrators under the age of 18. Note that our survey of victims cannot ascertain if this was the first occurrence of sexual abuse by the perpetrators.

Table 3.6 Age of Perpetrator	
20–29 years old	18.0%
30–39 years old	34.8%
40-49 years old	29.2%
50+ years old	18.0%

General population*: Average age early 30s, 33% under 18 years old
*Finkelhor 1994—19 studies

The 19-study summary indicated that among the "nonparental" category of abusers, one-third of the perpetrators were under the age of 18 (Finkelhor 1994). In a study that discusses the proportions of heterosexual versus homosexual perpetrators, Freund and Watson (1992) found that the mean age for perpetrators of children and at least one postpubescent victim were 37.3 years old against female victims and 34.6 against male children (37). Another study regarding personality characteristics of criminal sexual perpetrators places the mean age at 31.3 (Kalichman 1991:190).

By comparison, 47.2 percent of priest perpetrators are over the age of 40. Because of the *high* percentages in the 40+ age range, we question if the 34.8% represented in the 30–39 age group might be closer to 39 than 30.

In *A Sourcebook on Child Sexual Abuse* (1986), Finkelhor and Baron suggested that "victims were significantly more traumatized when abused by older (as opposed to younger) perpetrators" (173).

Discussion

Several scientists commonly use the term "ephebophilia" in their respective research on sexual abuse of adolescents, and as illustrated, the majority of the clergy abuse victims appear to fit that demo-graphic profile. Ephebophilia was coined by psycho-endocrinologist John Money of Johns Hopkins University (1980), and refers to un-wanted sexual contact and activities by adults with postpubescent adolescents—ages 14–19. While the term may not yet appear in any referenced dictionary, the related medical term, "ephebiatrics," does:

- Oxford's Dictionary Supplement: "The branch of medi-cine dealing with the study of adolescence and the diseases of young adults" (1993).
- Mosby's Medical, Nursing & Allied Health Dictionary: "branch of medicine that specializes in the health of ado-lescents" (Anderson, Anderson and Glanze 1994).

Researchers who have studied the priest perpetrator population in particular have found the term "ephebophilia" useful and significant:

- Psychotherapist A.W. Richard Sipe (1995): Ephebophiles: "men attracted to minors who have attained puberty" (14).
- Sociologist Philip Jenkins (1996): "Pedophile is a man sexually attracted to children below the age of puberty, but the vast majority of recorded instances of clergy 'abuse' or misconduct involve an interest in teenagers of either gen-der, often of fifteen or sixteen" (7).
- Sociologist Michael Crosby (1996): ". . . ephebophilia (a psy-chological term dealing with sexual or genital attraction to post-pubescent minors)" (94).
- Psychologist Stephen J. Rosetti (1994): "Most perpetrators of child sexual abuse are not pedophiles. Pedophilia is a clinical term referring to someone whose sexual orienta-tion is towards a pre-pubescent child. A minority of (priest) perpetrators of children are diagnosed pedophiles (10).

Why This Is Important: The Case for Ephebophilia

If a mother's son were a sexual perpetrator, she would want to know if he had a brain deficiency, as some researchers believe; if he had psychological problems, as other researchers believe; or if he hated women, as even other researchers believe. If that son were a priest, his mother would want to know if this was a pre-existing disease or condition, or whether something happened to him in the priesthood that might have caused the problem.

While a variety of research projects may have been done so far, there is frustration among contemporary and future students/scholars regarding the inability to compare statistics. More uniform methods have been suggested by several authors, as previously noted. This is especially important for treatment of both the victim and the perpetrator and also to establish preventive measures. With regard to the Catholic Church, it has been reported that a minimum of sixty thousand dollars per priest perpetrator is paid by a diocese for treatment. Between the financial settlements now said to be over a billion dollars and the psychological damage that has been done to victims and their families, it seems that new research methodologies need to be developed without delay.

Kalichman (1991), Ames and Houston (1990), and Greenberg, Bradford and Curry (1995), who have segregated study populations, all agree that the psychopathology differs among perpetrators of specific age victims. Kalichman recommends that perpetrator groups be separated in treatment and that different treatment methods be used . . . and in some instances that treatment approaches need to be combined. This could mean incarceration or treatment, incarceration *and* treatment, or even chemical castration for rapists as was proposed in the 1990s in California, as well as in the Philippines (AFP 1995).

On the one hand, APA (1994) recommends that criteria for statutes regarding mental disorders "explicitly include a diagnosed DSM-IV disorder involving significant impairment of impulse control relating to sexual behavior." On the other hand, they claim that all perpetrators except rapists are to be defined in different degrees as "pedophiles," a term clearly understood to mean prepubescent—under the biological age of adolescence. This can have devastating consequences regarding the treatment of perpetrators, not to mention the confusion that may come up in court cases and future research.

Conclusion

Based on the data presented, we conclude that the characteristics of Roman Catholic clergy sexual abuse are different from general population abuse. Our hypothesis, therefore, was supported.

DSM-IV-TR (2000) acknowledges various forms of "pedophile" sexual perpetrators such as heterosexual, homosexual, bisexual, regressed (attracted to children at times of stress), fixated (primarily attracted to prepubescent children), and incestual and nonincestual perpetrators. The concept of rape, also included in DSM-IV-TR, has reached a consensus among the disciplines and creates no confusion regarding related research *or* treatment *or* incarceration.

Since there are new definitions available and in common use among the research community regarding child sexual abuse, and since there is documentable evidence that not all child sexual abuse has the same characteristics, it seems appropriate to:

1. Accept and include the following as universal terminology in future printings of DSM to describe child sexual abuse, as well as in sociological and other scientific dictionaries and encyclopedias:

   A. *Infantophilia:* Sexual activity, whether physical or otherwise, with an infant child or children (generally age 0–5).

   B. *Pedophilia:* Sexual activity, whether physical or otherwise, with a prepubescent child or children (prepubescent/6–12[2]).

   C. *Ephebophilia:* Sexual activity, whether physical or otherwise, with a postpubescent or adolescent child or children (postpuberty/13–18).

   Until such time as the APA considers more suitable terminology to remedy the current confusion regarding the relevant concepts being discussed, we recommend that

---

[2] New data appearing in Magills Dictionary (Dawson 1998) speaks of "precocious puberty" beginning at ages 8 for girls and 9 for boys, where normal puberty onset is indicated for females between the ages of 10 and 12 and boys between the ages of 12 and 14. If this is adopted as the norm, it may place many more victims in the "ephebophilia" category.

the proposed distinctions of infantophilia, pedophilia, and ephebophilia be adopted by the scientific community at large so that future studies can be more reliable.

2. Subcategorize study populations for future research on child sexual abuse.

3. Use consistent methodology especially regarding demographics and peculiarities being studied.

If we put our conceptual house in order, we are more likely to be able to find useful scientific and factual results.

Bibliography

Abel, Gene G. and Joanne L. Rouleau. 1995. "Sexual abuses. Special Issue: Clinical sexuality." *Psychiatric Clinics of North America*, 1:139–153.

AFP. 1995. "Tough Pedophilia Bill Derailed." *International Herald Tribune*, November 8.

American Humane Association. 1996. *Fact Sheet*. Children's Division, AHA.

Ames, M. Ashley and David A. Houston. 1990. Legal, "Social, and Biological Definitions of Pedophilia." *Archives of Sexual Behavior*, 4:333–342.

Anderson, Kenneth N., Lois E. Anderson, and Walter D. Glanze. 1994. *Mosby's Medical, Nursing & Allied Health Dictionary*. St. Louis, MO: Mosby.

American Psychiatric Association: Diagnostic and Statistical Manual of Mental Disorders, DSM-IV-TR. 2000. Washington, D.C. APA.

———. 1994. *American Psychiatric Association: Diagnostic and Statistical Manual of Mental Disorders, DSM-IV*. Washington, D.C.: APA

———. 1987. *American Psychiatric Association: Diagnostic and Statistical Manual of Mental Disorders, DSM-IIIR*. Washington, D.C.: APA.

Bates, Frederick and Katherine S. van Wormer. 1979. "A Study of Leadership Roles in an Alabama Prison for Women." *Human Relations*. 9:793–801.

Briere, John and Marsha Runtz. 1989. "University Males' Sexual Interest in Children: Predicting Potential Indices of 'Pedophilia' in a Nonforensic Sample." *Child Abuse & Neglect.*13:65–75.

Burkett, Elixir and Frank Bruni. 1993. *Gospel of Shame.* NY: Penguin.

Cameron, P., W. Coburn, Jr., and H. Larson. 1986. "Child molestation and homosexuality." *Psychological Reports.* 58:327–37.

Coridin, James A., Thomas G. Green, and Donald E. Heintschel. 1985. *The Code of Canon Law. A text and commentary.* Mahwah, NJ: Paulist Press.

Crosby, Michael H. 1996. *Celibacy—Means of Control or Mandate of the Heart?* Notre Dame, IN: Ave Maria Press.

Dabrow, Allan M. 1970. "Comment—The Pros and Cons of Conjugal Visits in Prison Institutions." *Journal of Family Law.* 9:436–440.

Oxford Dictionary, The. 1989. Simpson, J.A. and E. S. C. Weiner. Oxford: Clarendon Press.

Finkelhor, David. 1994. "Current Information on the Scope and Nature of Child Sexual Abuse." *The Future of Children. Sexual Abuse of Children.* 2:31–53.

———. 1989. "Early and Long-term Effects of Child Sexual Abuse: An Update." *Professional Psychology: Research and Practice.* 21:325–330.

Finkelhor, David and Sharon Araji. 1986. "Explanations of Pedophilia: A four factor model." *Journal of Sexual Research.* 22:145–161.

Finkelhor, David and L. Baron. 1986. "High-risk Children." Pp. 60–88 in *A Sourcebook on Child Sexual Abuse.* Edited by D. Finkelhor. Beverly Hills, CA: Sage.

Finkelhor, David, G. Hotaling, I.A. Lewis and C. Smith. 1990. "Sexual Abuse in a National Survey of Adult Men and Women: Prevalence, Characteristics, and Risk Factors." *Child Abuse & Neglect.* 14:19–28.

Finkelhor, David and Lisa Jones. 2004. "Explanations for the decline in child sexual abuse cases." *Office of Juvenile Justice and Delinquency Prevention/OJJDP Juvenile Justice Bulletin,* January 2004. [Online] Retrieved February 27, 2004.

Freund, Kurt and Robin Watson. 1992. "The Proportions of Heterosexual and Homosexual Pedophiles among Sex Offenders against Children: An Exploratory Study." *Journal of Sex & Marital Therapy.* 1:34–43.

Gifis, Steven H. 1996. *Law Dictionary.* Happauge, NY: Barron's.

Gosselin, Henry. 1996. Who's Sitting in the Pews? *Church World.* 35:4

Greenberg, David M., John Bradford, and Susan Curry. 1995. "Infantophilia—A New Subcategory of Pedophilia? A Preliminary Study." *Bull American Academy Psychiatry Law.* 1:63–70.

Groth, Nicholas A., William F. Hobson, and Thomas S. Gary. 1982. *The Child Molester: Clinical Observations.* NY: Barron's.

Grubin, Don. 1992. "Sexual Offending: a cross-cultural comparison." *Annual Review of Sex Research.* (3)201–217.

Haggett, Louise. 2000. "Is a sexually abusing Roman Catholic priest a pedophile? The case for ephebophilia." Presented at the 70th Annual Meeting of the Eastern Sociological Society, Baltimore Hilton, Baltimore, March 2–5.

———. 1999. ibid. Presented at the Society for the Scientific Study of Religion and Religious Research Association's *"What Do We Know about Religious Institutions and How Have We Come to Know It?"* Swissotel, Boston, November 5–7.

Jenkins, Philip. 1996. *Pedophiles and priests. Anatomy of a Contemporary Crisis.* NY: Oxford University Press.

Kalichman, Seth C. 1991. "Psychopathology and Personality Characteristics of Criminal Sexual Offenders as a Function of Victim Age." *Archives of Sexual Behavior.* 2:187–197.

Kendall-Tackett, K.A., L. M. Williams, and D. Finkelhor. 1993. "Impact of Sexual Abuse on Children: A Review and Synthesis of recent Empirical Studies." *Psychological Bulletin* 113:164–180.

Kercher, Glen A. and Marilyn McShane. 1984. "The Prevalence of Child Sexual Abuse Victimization in an Adult Sample of Texas Residents." *Child Abuse & Neglect.* 8:495–501.

Lynch, Gerald W., Michele Galietta, Margaret Leland Smith, James Levine, Maureen O'Connor, Steven Penrod, Louis Schlesinger, Karen Terry. 2004 *The Nature and Scope of Sexual Abuse of Minors*

by Catholic Priests and Deacons in the United States 1950– 2002.
NY: The John Jay College of Criminal Justice.

Magills Dictionary. 1998. Edited by D. Dawson. Westerville, OH:
Hans & Cassidy.

Money, John. 1980. *Love and Love Sickness.* Baltimore: Johns Hopkins University Press.

Moore, K., C. Nord, and J. Peterson. 1989. "Nonvoluntary Sexual
Activity among Adolescents. *Family Planning Perspectives."*
21:110–14.

Morris, Charles R. 1997. *American Catholic.* NY: Vintage.

Oxford Dictionary, The. 1989. J.A. Simpson and E.S.C. Weiner, editors. Oxford, England: Clarendon Press.

Peters, S.D., G.E. Wyatt, and D. Finkelhor. 1986. "Prevalence."
Pp. 15–59 in *A Sourcebook on Child Sexual Abuse,* edited by
D. Finkelhor. Beverly Hills, CA: Sage.

Rich, Vera. 1999. "Marry now . . . or not at all." *London Tablet,*
October 23.

Rossetti, Stephen J. 1994. "Priests Suicides and the Crisis of Faith."
America Magazine, October 29.

Rothenberg, Robert E. 1995. *The Plain Language Law Dictionary.*
NY: Penguin.

Russell, D. 1983. "The Incidence and Prevalence of Intrafamilial and
Extrafamilial Sexual Abuse of Female Children." *Child Abuse &*
Neglect. 7:133–146.

Sedlak, A. 1991. *National Incidence and Prevalence of Child Abuse*
and Neglect:1988. Revised Report. Rockville, MD: Westat.

Sipe, A.W. Richard. 1995. *Sex, Priests and Power: Anatomy of a Crisis.*
NY: Brunner /Mazel.

———. 1990. *A Secret World: Sexuality and the Search for Celibacy.*
NY: Brunner /Mazel.

Thomas, Judy. 2000. "Report Explores AIDS, Priests." *Associated Press*
in Kansas City Star. Kansas City, MO., January 29.
(http//www.kcstar.com/item/pages/home.pat,local/37743133.129.,html).
Retrieved January 20, 2000.

Merriam Webster's Dictionary of Law. 1996. Springfield, MA: Merriam Webster.

Webster's Seventh New Collegiate Dictionary. 1969. Springfield, MA: Merriam Webster.

Wyld, Henry Cecil & Partridge Eric H. 1969. *Complete and Unabridged the Little & Ives Webster Dictionary.* NY: J.J. Little & Ives Co.

Zonana, H., Gene Abel, John Bradford, Steven Hoge and Jeffrey Melzner. 1998. *APA Task Force Report on Sexually Dangerous Offenders.* Unpublished.

4

Is Sexual Abuse by Roman Catholic Clergy Only About Child Sexual Abuse?

An Adult Study

C lergy sexual abuse does not end when victims reach age 17. In fact, clergy sexual abuse of adult victims produces quite different distributions demographically from clergy sexual abuse of minors, with regard to both victim and perpetrator profiles. Adult abuse is also the only area where our data compare to general societal abuse, a claim many associates within the church have made about *all* clergy sexual abuse.

On February 27, 2004, the highly publicized John Jay College Study entitled "The Nature and Scope of Sexual Abuse of Minors by Catholic Priests and Deacons in the United States, 1950–2002" was released to the general public during a major news conference in Washington, D.C., and later through a "Town Meeting" format on Catholic Television's EWTN Network (Arroyo 2004). Commissioned by the U.S. Conference of Catholic Bishops, the John Jay College Study was a self-audit of as many of the U.S. dioceses as were willing to participate (195 out of 202 eligible). The survey was also sent to the 221 religious orders of men, out of which 133 were returned. (Lynch et al. 2004)

The John Jay College Study, however, included only victims up to the age of 17 where the demographic majority is male. During the question/answer period in the telecast, when asked why the study was only on victims who were minors, a spokesperson for the National Review Board replied that it was "outside our purview (authority) to investigate the questions of priests having sex with adults."

One example of John Jay College's limited study, for instance, listed only four bishops as accused perpetrators as of December 2002, the time period when the John Jay College study ended. Had they included bishops who have abused adults, the figure of accused bishops by the previous June 2002 would have been 12 (Egerton and Dunklin 2002: 27A). As of August 2004, at least 15 bishops had been accused of sexual abuse (CST online 2004). If we applied that percentage difference to the rest of the clergy perpetrators, we would be looking at an incidence figure of much higher than the reported 6 percent, bringing up the question of age and perhaps gender of the victims over 17 years of age.

Another reason for the adult section of the Victim Study is to call into question unsubstantiated statements that Catholic clergy sexual abuse is a homosexual problem. When the Center for the Study of Religious Issues (CSRI) conducted its study of Roman Catholic clergy abuse victims in 1999, we were under the impression that the majority of victims of clergy abuse were minors. For this reason, our sampling was compared to the general population studies of child sexual abuse. However, the response rate to the CSRI study among those victimized as adults was so significant (31.3 percent) that it warrants presenting the findings separately.

The relevant tables that were limited to adolescent victims in chapter 3 have been reconfigured for this section to include *all* responses received from clergy sexual abuse victims in our 1999 study. Not only was there a large number of victims at age 19 or over, *but beyond 20 years old, there was a dramatic shift from male to female victims—94.5 percent females and 5.5 percent males versus 93% male in the adolescent category..*

This section of the Victim Study reviews findings regarding adult victims (>19) of clergy sexual abuse. Note that the CSRI numbers included the age of 18 as part of the "minors" statistics because 18 years old was the cut-off age in the majority of studies reported in Finkelhor's 19-study summary on child sexual abuse. These demographics therefore cannot be separated to make comparisons with the John Jay Study demographics, which end at age 17, because of the methodology used in the CSRI questionnaire. We believe that if age 18 were included in the adult percentages, the adult data might be even more significant.

Notice the dramatic change in the gender of the majority of victims of priests as the victims get older. This makes us wonder if priests, when they first become sexually active, choose inexperienced male adolescents who may be more closely related to their own psychosexual development, consistent with Fr. Connors' remarks at the 1993 NFPC conference in which we said, "If girls are off limits, maybe boys are okay," (chapter 1) and who may be the easier target, as some psychologists have indicated. Then, as priest perpetrators become more experienced and/or have new opportunities, they choose adult female victims. The other option for the mystery of opposite genders would be two different types of perpetrators. In fact, adult abuse presents the *only* correlation present in our data that provides a similar pattern in Catholic clergy sexual abuse to that of sexual abuse by other denominational clergy.

Table 4.1	Age and Gender of Victims			
Age at Victimization	Victims of Priests under 18 (%)		All Victims of Priests (%)	
	Male	Female	Male	Female
0–6 years old	0.0%	19.1%	0.0%	12.2%
7–9 years old	9.4%	25.5%	8.8%	16.2%
10–13 years old	50.9%	25.5%	47.4%	16.2%
14–15 years old	32.1%	10.6%	29.8%	6.8%
16–18* years old	7.5%	19.1%	7.0%	12.2%
19 years old	0.0%	0.0%	5.3%	5.4%
20+ years old	0.0%	0.0%	1.8%	31.1%

Chi square: .0001

*The age category breakdown in the CSRI study was 16–18; therefore percentages for >17 are not available.

There is hardly any research on other denominational sexual abuse from which we can make comparisons to Catholic clergy abuse. One study conducted in 1994 confirmed our hypothesis that the demographics of child sexual abuse by Roman Catholic clergy are different from other denominational abuse. According to Barbara McLaughlin (1994), who studied the spiritual impact of clergy sexual abuse, "All the Protestant survivors [among her study population] were abused as adults," and "all Protestant survivors were women" (1994:149–150). Our data indicate that adult victims (>19) of Catholic clergy comprise 84 percent females and 16 percent males.

Tables 4.2 to 4.5 show very little variation between gender and adolescents and adults in terms of the duration and form of abuse. Duration of abuse by Catholic clergy, as previously stated, differs from societal abuse, at least among those 18 years old and under.

Table 4.2	Duration of Abuse by Gender				
Victims	I time only*	I month or less	I–6 months	6 months –I year	More than I year
Male <18	20.8%	7.5%	17.0%	9.4%	45.3%
Female <18	13.6%	2.3%	2.3%	11.4%	70.4%
Male >19	22.8%	10.5%	15.8%	8.8%	42.4%
Female >19	15.5%	4.2%	4.2%	9.9%	66.3%

Chi Square: .048
*One-time-only abuse among the general population: 68.5%

Table 4.3   Duration of Abuse/Age of Victim at Onset

I time	I month only*	I–6 or less	6 months months	More than –I year	I year
0–6 years old	12.5%	0.0%	12.5%	0.0%	75.0%
7–9 years old	13.3%	0.0%	0.0%	6.7%	80.0%
10–13 years old	23.1%	10.3%	10.3%	2.6%	53.8%
14–15 years old	9.1%	4.5%	22.7%	13.6%	49.9%
16–18 years old	23.1%	0.0%	0.0%	38.5%	38.5%
19 years old	14.3%	28.6%	0.0%	14.3%	42.9%
20+ years old	25.0%	8.3%	8.3%	4.2%	54.2%

*One-time-only abuse among the general population: 68.5%

Table 4.4   Form of Abuse

Victims	No Physical Contact	Some physical contact	Primarily Physical	Physical/ nonphysical
Victims <18	1.0%	.0%	24.0%	74.0%
Victims >19	1.5%	4.6%	22.9%	71.0%

Table 4.5   Form of Abuse/Victim Age at Onset

Victims	No Physical Contact	Some physical contact	Primarily Physical	Physical/ nonphysical
0–6 years old	0.0%	11.1%	22.2%	66.7%
7–9 years old	5.9%	0.0%	29.4%	64.7%
10–13 years old	0.0%	0.0%	30.8%	69.2%
14–15 years old	0.0%	0.0%	13.6%	86.4%
16–18 years old	0.0%	0.0%	15.4%	84.6%
19 years old	0.0%	14.3%	28.6%	57.1%
20+ years old	4.2%	16.7%	16.7%	62.5%

While the word "penetration" was not used in the Haggett 1999 study regarding "form of abuse," the 19-study summary concluded "the longer the abuse, the more chance for penetration . . . and the longer the abuse, the more psychological damage" (Finkelhor 1994).

Discussion

The John Jay College Report made no mention of a possible homosexual factor; however, that unfounded conclusion was drawn by others during the EWTN telecast in relation to the study as a potential cause of clergy sexual abuse. Since the study, Vatican officials as well as individual bishops have issued control regulations regarding the acceptance of gays in some seminaries.

Research that has been conducted regarding sexual abuse in prison systems indicates that lack of normal sexual release in same-sex institutional systems can lead to homosexual activity among heterosexuals. Several studies were conducted regarding deviant sexual activity in both men's and women's prisons in the 1960s and 1970s (Ibrahim 1974, van Wormer and Bates 1979, Sullivan 1970, Ward and Kassebaum 1964). Ward reported that the prevalence of homosexual behavior among the general public was 13 percent versus 69 percent in prisons and that 90 percent of the prisoners who engaged in homosexual activity in prisons began that practice in the prison system (167). He further reported that, "Prison homosexuality, even by many of those involved was regarded as temporary, with heterosexual relations to be resumed upon release."(164).

According to Christopher Hensley (2001) of the Institute for Correction Research & Training in Kentucky, "Men immersed in single-sex environments, such as boarding schools, the military, remote work sites, and correctional institutions, have long been known to engage in sexual activities with one another, yet staunchly maintain a heterosexual identity. Sexual activities with other men are defined as simply a response to the deprivation or a lack of mixed-sex interactions. General belief holds that most men engaged in situational same-sex activities would return to heterosexual sexual activities once removed from the segregated environment" (61). In an earlier study, Hensley wrote, "Most men that participate in homosexual behavior usually come into prison with a heterosexual identity" (1997: 46). Gary Thomas Long (1993) suggested that, "The writings about *homosexuality* in prison would perhaps be better described as about *homosexual behavior* in prison, inferring that these are not homosexuals, but rather heterosexuals engaging in homosexual behavior—an important distinction" (145). Other studies concur (French, 1979, Nacci and Kane 1983, 1984, Diamant 1993).

Hensley also related statistics from Laud Humphreys' monumental study on homosexuality, "Tearoom Trade" (1975), in which Humphreys stated that among the cases he surveyed of heterosexual men performing homosexual acts, 63 percent were Catholic husbands who said their conjugal relations were rare. While Humphreys' population sample was an unstructured collectivity of individuals, his data indicated "diminished intercourse plus religious teachings may have in some way combined to cause the husband to search for [homosexual] sex in the tearooms" (Hensley 1997:28). The "boys are okay" scenario (Connors, 1993) seemed to work here also, perhaps because there would be less emotional involvement for these men in this type of sexual activity than in a heterosexual affair. The subject of sexual abstinence among male Catholics in general is different from the study at hand, but it serves to demonstrate that forced abstinence can lead to deviance.

In 1990, noted celibacy-researcher psychotherapist A. W. Richard Sipe claimed an incidence factor of 30 percent homosexuality in the priesthood, "about double that of the general population" (71). He added, however, "Not all homosexual contact between priests and adolescents involves a man who is of an obligatory homosexual orientation" (169), a conclusion drawn from both prison research as well as "Tearoom Trade," as previously noted.

A 1996 study of "clerics vs. non-clerics" by Haywood et al. concluded that Catholic priests were more likely to have "older victims and victims of male gender than non-clerical alleged child molesters" (527). While we found this to be true for a higher percentage than normal in the Adolescent Study (chapter 3), the significant number of female victims both among minors and adults is different. We therefore conclude that gay priests are not the cause nor were they a major factor in the problem, at least in the majority of cases that took place in the 1980s and prior.

It would seem if homosexuality were the only issue among priest/perpetrators, that as a priest aged, the sexual abuse among adult male victims would remain as high as it was between 10- to 16-year-old victims. Table 4.1 clearly shows a gender change from male to female victims of clergy sexual abuse after the age of 20. The over-20 CSRI incidence for male victims was only 1.8 percent. The high percentage of adult female victims (31.1 percent), however, provides evidence of a high incidence of heterosexual abuse by Catholic priest/perpetrators, perhaps the only factor in the clergy abuse phenomenon that mirrors societal abuse and similar to other denominational clergy who occasionally prey on adult women.

Another more logical argument that the majority of clergy sexual perpetrators are not intrinsically homosexual is that if they were, they would not have to go outside their own walls to find homosexual intimacy (Sipe 1990). While there may be a high rate of homosexuals in the Roman Catholic priesthood today, we conclude that the issue of clergy sexual abuse is not primarily a homosexual issue, at least not in the majority of earlier cases. Our data also indicate that clergy sexual abuse, by significant numbers, does not end with adolescents (41 out of 131 respondents >19).

Bibliography

Arroyo, Raymond, narrator. 2004. "National Review Board Report on Clergy Sexual Abuse." EWTN Television Network, February 27.

Connors, Fr. Canice. 1993. "The Issue of Sexual Misconduct & the Clergy." Workshop presented at the 15th Annual National Federation of Priests Council (NFPC) Convention & House of Delegates. Chicago, IL, May.

CST. 2004. "Bishops accused of sexual misconduct." *(http://www.WFAA.com/s/dws/spe/2002/-bishops/stories/061202dnmetbishide.1d 915.html)*.

Diamant, Louis. 1993. *Homosexual issues in the workplace*. Philadelphia, PA: Taylor & Francis.

Egerton, Brooks, Reese Dunklin. 2002. "Bishops accused of sexual misconduct." *The Dallas Morning News,* June 12.

Finkelhor, David. 1994. "Current Information on the Scope and Nature of Child Sexual Abuse." *The Future of Children. Sexual Abuse of Children*. 4:31–53.

French, Laurence. 1979. "Prison Sexualization: Inmate Adaptations to Psycho-sexual Stress." *Corrective & Social Psychiatry & Journal of Behavior Technology, Methods & Therapy.* 25:64–69.

Haggett, Louise. 2000. "Is A Sexual Abusing Roman Catholic Priest a Pedophile? The Case for Ephebophilia." Presented at the 70th Annual Meeting of the Eastern Sociological Society, Baltimore Hilton, Baltimore, March 2–5.

———. 1999 "Is a Sexual Abusing Roman Catholic Priest a Pedophile? The Case for Ephebophilia." Presented at the Society for the Scientific Study of Religion and Religious Research Association's *What Do We Know about Religious Institutions and How Have We Come to Know It?"* Swissotel, Boston, November 5–7.

Haywood, Thomas W., Howard M. Kravitz, Linda S. Grossman, Orest E. Wasylow, Daniel W. Hardy. 1996. "Psychological Aspects of Sexual Functioning Among Cleric and Non-Cleric Alleged Sex Offenders." *Child Abuse & Neglect.* 20:527–536.

Hensley, Christopher. 2001. "Exploring the Dynamics of Masturbation and Consensual Same-Sex Activity within a Male Maximum Security Prison." *The Journal of Men's Studies.* 1:59–71.

———.1997. "From Behind the Walls of Confinement: an Analysis of Mississippi Prisoners' Attitude toward Sexuality." *Dissertation Abstracts International Section A: Humanities & Social Sciences.* 58:2857.

Humphreys, Laud. 1970, 1975. *Tearoom Trade. Impersonal sex in public places*. Hawthorne, NY: Aldine de Gruyter.

Ibrahim, Azmy Ishal. 1974. "Deviant Sexual Behavior in Men's Prisons." *Crime and Delinquency.* 20:38–44.

Long, Gary Thomas. 1993. "Homosexual Relationships in a Unique Setting: The Male Prison." *Homosexual Issues in the Workplace*, edited by Louis Diamant. 8:143–159.

Lynch, Gerald W., Michele Galietta, Margaret Leland Smith, James Levine, Maureen O'Connor, Steven Penrod, Louis Schlesinger, Karen Terry. 2004 *The Nature and Scope of Sexual Abuse of Minors by Catholic Priests and Deacons in the United States 1950–2002*. NY: The John Jay College of Criminal Justice.

McLaughlin, Barbara R. 1994. "Devastated Spirituality: The Impact of Clergy Sexual Abuse on the Survivor's Relationship with God and the Church." *Sexual Addiction & Compulsivity.*

Nacci, Peter L., Thomas R. Kane. 1984. Inmate Sexual Aggression: Some Evolving Propositions, Empirical Findings, and Mitigating Counter-forces. *Journal of Offender Counseling, Services & Rehabilitation. Special Issue: Gender issues, sex offenses, and criminal justice: Current trends.* 9:1–20.

————. 1983. "The Incidence of Sex and Sexual Aggression in Federal Prisons." *Federal Probation.* 47:31–36.

Sipe, A. W. Richard. 2003. *Celibacy in Crisis. A Secret World Revisited.* NY: Brunner Routledge.

————. 1995. *Sex, Priests and Power. Anatomy of a Crisis.* NY: Brunner Mazel.

————. 1990. *A Secret World: Sexuality and the Search for Celibacy.* NY: Brunner Mazel.

Sullivan, Richard. 1970. "Comment—The Pros and Cons of Conjugal Visits in Prison Institutions." *Journal of Family Law.* 9:436–440.

Van Wormer, Katherine, Frederick L. Bates. 1979. "A Study of Leadership Roles in an Alabama Prison for Women." *Human Relations.* 32:793–801.

Ward, David A. and Gene G. Kassebaum. 1964. "Homosexuality: A Mode of Adaptation in a Prison for Women." *Social Problems.* 159–177.

5

When Was Abuse Reported?
What Were the Priest's Needs?

T he question, "When was abuse reported?" is relevant in 2004 for two reasons: (1) the revealing statistic from the Priest Study in chapter 2 noting that the church disciplined priest/perpetrators only when the abuse became public knowledge, and (2) report on the history of child sexual abuse among the general public that differs greatly from clergy abuse. (Finkelhor et al. 1990)

As early as 1993, the Wall Street Journal reported countersuits by the Catholic Church against victims of clergy sexual abuse. According to WSJ, there were wiretaps of victims' phones and other harassing measures to get them to drop charges against their perpetrators or the church. (Geyelin 1993:A48). This publicized activity on the part of the church may have discouraged other victims from coming forward with their claims.

One variable discussed in the 1990 child sexual abuse study by Finkelhor et al. measured the length of time it took victims among the general population to tell anyone about their abuse. They were asked if they told "within one year," or "yes, later," or "no, never." A similar question was asked in the Haggett 1999 Victim Study, but with different options: "at the time," "within six months" "7 months to 2 years," 3–10 years," "11–20 years," "20 or more years" and "no, never." Results appear in Table 5.1 on following page.

Table 5.1 observations: The younger the victim, the longer it took to tell anyone. Generally speaking in terms of the minors, the findings are inconsistent with a Finkelhor child abuse study (1990) in which the question "Did you tell anyone?" produced a 42 percent average response of telling anyone within one year of the abuse. The highest percentage among priest victims under 19 years of age who told any-one within two years was 16.6 percent.

It was surprising to see that over 17 percent of the CSRI Victim Study respondents still had not reported their abuse as of 1999, even though they had already connected with the support organization Linkup. Yet 76.7 percent of these signed our questionnaire, an optional action. A few of the respondents indicated that their healing began just through their participation in our survey, and thirteen respondents thanked CSRI for initiating the study.

One would think that once a survivor joins an organization that can help promote healing, the victim would be more apt to want to talk about it. Perhaps the shame of telling and fear of not being believed prevented many from making it public thus far. Six respondents reported having "told" twice, years apart because no one believed them the first time. One might conclude, therefore, that while the suppression or "gag" monies reportedly paid to victims in many instances by the Catholic Church may serve to cover up the crimes of the past, this very act may have exacerbated the psychological damage already done.

A significant finding was in the subsequent question, "To Whom Was It Reported?" The significance is not so much the specific individual who was told as much as the number of people he or she told. It was as though once the secret was out, the rest of the world must know.

The consistencies between the victim responses in Table 5.2, and priests acknowledging that the Church was aware of the problem

Table 5.1 When Was Abuse Reported?

Age	When Abuse Happened	Within 2 yrs	3–10 Yrs	11–20 Yrs	20+ Yrs	Never	Reported Twice*
0–6 years old	11.1%	0.0%	0.0%	0.0%	55.6%	22.2%	11.1%
7–9 years old	5.9%	0.0%	0.0%	5.9%	52.9%	29.4%	5.9%
10–13 years old	0.0%	2.8%	13.9%	16.7%	47.2%	16.7%	2.8%
14–15 years old	4.5%	13.6%	9.1%	13.6%	45.5%	4.5%	9.1%
16–18 years old	0.0%	15.4%	15.4%	23.1%	30.8%	15.4%	0.0%
19 years old	0.0%	33.4%	0.0%	16.7%	33.3%	16.7%	0.0%
20+ years old	0.0%	41.7%	25.0%	0.0%	8.3%	20.8%	4.2%

*Reported twice, years in between (disbelief the first time)

Gamma: -.254; p<.006

Table 5.2	To Whom Was Abuse Reported? (All Victims)
Pastor	9%
Another priest	5.4%
Bishop	6.3%
Other school/church official	7.2%
Legal authorities	9%
Professionals (counselors, etc.)	9.9%
Parents	2.7%
Media	9%
Told 2 to 4 people	46.8%
Told 5 or more people	18.9%

from the Priests' Study in chapter 1 strengthens the evidence that the Church officials were aware that abuse of some of their parishioners was taking place and that they were ignoring the problem altogether. The following table (5.3) repeats statistics in Table 5.2 with an age breakdown to illustrate the pattern, leading us to conclude that the church neither disciplined priests, as noted in chapter 2, nor did they assist the victims.

Victims Speak about Their Priest Perpetrators

The majority of adolescent victims of Roman Catholic clergy perpetrators were believed to be male altar servers. The question "How Did You Know Offender?" revealed a different characteristic among adult survivors, however. Table 5.4 indicates that a significant percentage of 16- to18-year-olds as well as the majority of 20+-year-olds encountered their priest perpetrator in a counseling or employee/employer atmosphere. *This is the only instance in the entire Bingo Report where Roman Catholic clergy sexual abuse demographics can be compared to sexual abuse in other religious denominations where most*

Table 5.3 | To Whom Was Abuse Reported?/Age of Victim at Onset

Age	Another Pastor	Church Priest	Bishop	Official	Legal	Prof.	Parents	Media	# of People 2–4	5+
0–6 yrs. old	0.0%	0.0%	0.0%	0.0%	0.0%	25.0%	12.5%	0.0%	37.5%	25.0%
7–9 yrs. old	7.7%	7.7%	7.7%	0.0%	0.0%	7.7%	0.0%	0.0%	46.2%	23.1%
10–13 yrs. old	0.0%	3.1%	9.4%	9.4%	3.1%	6.3%	3.1%	3.1%	40.6%	21.9%
14–15 yrs. old	0.0%	9.1%	9.1%	4.5%	0.0%	9.1%	4.5%	0.0%	54.5%	9.1%
16–18 yrs. old	0.0%	0.0%	0.0%	9.1%	0.0%	18.2%	0.0%	0.0%	63.5%	9.1%
19 yrs. old	0.0%	0.0%	0.0%	20.0%	0.0%	20.0%	0.0%	0.0%	60.0%	0.0%
20+ yrs. old	0.0%	10.0%	5.0%	10.0%	0.0%	5.0%	0.0%	0.0%	40.0%	30.0%

Table 5.4 How Did Victim Know Perpetrator?/Age of Victim at Onset

Age	Was altar server	Abused by counselor	Abused by teacher	Youth group	Seminary	Family Friend	Convert	Employee
0–6 yrs. old	0.0%	11.1%	11.1%	11.1%	0.0%	66.7%	0.0%	0.0%
7–9 yrs. old	17.6%	11.8%	11.8%	5.9%	0.0%	47.1%	0.0%	5.9%
10–13 yrs. old	43.6%	2.6%	7.7%	17.9%	2.6%	23.1%	0.0%	2.6%
14–15 yrs. old	36.4%	18.2%	18.2%	4.5%	9.1%	13.6%	0.0%	0.0%
16–18 yrs. old	0.0%	46.2%	15.4%	15.4%	7.7%	7.7%	0.0%	7.7%
19 yrs. old	0.0%	28.6%	14.3%	14.3%	0.0%	28.6%	14.3%	0.0%
20+ yrs. old	0.0%	54.2%	4.2%	0.0%	0.0%	12.5%	4.2%	25.0%

Chi Square: .0001

perpetrators are married clergy, or where the abuse is in the same arena as sexual harassment in corporate society. Relative to married clergy, the John Jay College Report indicated a 1 percent abuse factor among married deacons (1.0 percent), and there are over 13,000 married deacons in the Catholic Church.

A study of this older group of victims might reveal a different type of perpetrator among the Catholic clergy; or a priest/perpetrator who abused both adolescents and adults. Researching the respective offenders' files to compare names of perpetrators and ages of victims might uncover the details. Without access to diocesan files, however, it is difficult to make that determination.

We attempted to ascertain how much the victims knew about their priest perpetrator. Since the majority endured the abuse for a long period of time, they probably got to know their perpetrator well. When asked, "Is he still a priest?" only 15.3 percent said yes, 26.0 percent said no, 12.2 percent indicated that he was deceased, and the remaining 46.5 percent either did not know or did not answer. Other questions more pertinent to the time period during which the respondents were abused asked about the perpetrator's approximate age, the number of years he had been an ordained priest, and what they felt were his needs. While it is understood that minors might not understand the underlying meanings of these terms if these questions were asked while they were still minors, such questions would be appropriate and significant in a retrospective study, according to Finkelhor (1994).

There was very little difference in responses from adolescent versus adult victims regarding the age of the clergy perpetrator. The middle range (30–49 years of age) represented 64 percent of perpetrators of adolescent victims and when combined with adult victims, 53.3%. As previously mentioned, because of the high percentage of clergy perpetrators over 40 years of age (29.2 percent) compared to the average general public perpetrator (early 30s), we interpret the 30–39 perpetrator age factor to be closer to 39 than 30 among priests.

Table 5.5 | Age of Perpetrator/Victim Age at Onset

| | Age of Perpetrator | | | |
	20–29 years old	30–39 years old	40–49 years old	50+ years old
0–6 years old	33.3%	33.3%	16.7%	16.7%
7–9 years old	14.3%	35.7%	21.4%	28.6%
10–13 years old	20.0%	37.1%	20.0%	22.9%
14–15 years old	18.2%	31.8%	45.5%	4.5%
16–18 years old	8.3%	33.3%	41.7%	16.7%
19 years old	14.3%	28.6%	28.6%	28.6%
20+ years old	8.3%	16.7%	37.5%	37.5%

Gamma: .204; p<.040

As previously indicated, Finkelhor and Baron (1986) wrote, "Victims were significantly more traumatized when abused by older (as opposed to younger) perpetrators" (173).

The responses to the victim question, "What were his needs?" shown in Table 5.6 brought out into the open the latent variable[1]—*loneliness*—that has surfaced in most general studies on mandatory celibacy, as discussed in the Literary Study that follows. Again, this question and the percentages that follow would have been less significant if (1) they had been asked of a minor and (2) did not coincide with other studies on mandatory celibacy.

The optional responses in Table 5.6 "What Were His Needs?" were defined as follows in the survey instrument:

- Biological (natural sexual need)
- Emotional (loneliness)
- Authoritarian (abuse of power)
- Other *(please explain)*_____

Respondents were asked to check all that applied, the reason for the combined answers in Table 5.6.

Mental problems was a write-in response under "Other—please explain." Respondents were asked retrospectively, to check off as many "needs" as applied; the reason for the combined responses that were added after tabulation took place because of significant percentages therein.

It is common knowledge that a large percentage of clergy victims/survivors today hate not just their perpetrators, but all priests as a result of their abuse. Yet, over 50 percent of the survivor respondents acknowledged that the needs their perpetrator(s) had included biological (natural sexual need) and emotional (loneliness). This is consistent with an important component cited in the Priest Study in the breaking of vows: loneliness and the need for intimacy (close relationship). Loneliness is discussed in detail in the next chapter.

---

[1] Latent variable: an underlying variable that was not included in either questionnaire, but appeared in enough responses to consider it reliable.

Table 5.6	What Were His Needs?/Age of Victim At Onset							
Age	Biological	Emotional	Authoritarian	Bio/Emo	Emo/Auth	Bio/Emo/Auth	Bio/Auth	Mental Probl.
0–6 yrs. old	0.0%	0.0%	16.7%	0.0%	16.7%	16.7%	0.0%	50.0%
7–9 years old	10.0%	0.0%	30.0%	10.0%	10.0%	20.0%	0.0%	20.0%
10–13 years old	7.7%	3.8%	38.5%	7.7%	7.7%	3.8%	7.7%	23.1%
14–15 years old	5.6%	5.6%	22.2%	11.1%	11.1%	27.8%	5.6%	11.1%
16–18 years old	7.7%	7.7%	23.1%	7.7%	15.4%	15.4%	0.0%	23.1%
19 years old	16.7%	16.7%	33.3%	16.7%	0.0%	0.0%	0.0%	16.7%
20+ years old	8.3%	8.3%	29.2%	12.5%	8.3%	12.5%	8.3%	12.5%

Bibliography

Finkelhor, David. 1994. "Current Information on the Scope and Nature of Child Sexual Abuse." *The Future of Children. Sexual Abuse of Children.* 4:31–53.

Finkelhor, David, G. Hotaling, I.A. Lewis and C. Smith. 1990. "Sexual Abuse in a National Survey of Adult Men and Women: Prevalence, Characteristics and Risk Factors." *Child Abuse and Neglect.* 14:19–28.

Geyelin, Milo. 1993. "The Catholic Church Struggles with Suits over Sexual Abuse." *Wall Street Journal,* November 24.

Haggett, Louise, Tara Hanson, Megan Solo. 1997. "What Factors Contribute to Catholic Priests Breaking Their Vows of Celibacy/ Chastity?" Unpublished.

Lynch, Gerald W., Michele Galietta, Margaret Leland Smith, James Levine, Maureen O'Connor, Steven Penrod, Louis Schlesinger, Karen Terry. 2004 *"The Nature and Scope of Sexual Abuse of Minors by Catholic Priests and Deacons in the United States 1950– 2002."* NY: The John Jay College of Criminal Justice.

CSRI Comments [sic]

Codes: Letter "M" or "F" after number indicates male or female.
Letter "U" or "S" after comment indicates unsigned or signed.
Names of priests/bishops/dioceses have been omitted.

#003M—Told parents at the time it happened. They wouldn't believe me. Students at (boarding) school, seeing me singled out by the priest, gang raped me in the tunnel and threatened my life if I told anyone. No one truly knows, unless experienced, how this unbalances the mind, turns one off to clerics and God and how one can be tormented the rest of one's life by the urges towards the males the same as when you, yourself were violated. It is more than a sexual urge—it is anger, frustration, rage and an urge to lash out and harm those young males who are turning on your sex urges against your will. I haven't turned into a molester but have to fight the compulsion even though I steer clear of certain situations with seeing the young males. U

#004F—Are you aware of any support advocacy groups or counselors who were abused as children (rate of correlation abuse=career in social, etc. work)? S

#005F—I resent all clergy perpetrators and any person and/or institution that protects them and covers up for them. I will never understand nor accept clergy sexual abuse and exploitation, but I know it exists and know the lasting devastation it causes the victims. S

#007F—Sexual contact is different and more intrusive than just physical contact—it was rape and needs to be named as such. Both my brothers were sexually abused by a priest (different from mine) who was assistant pastor at the church for brothers. Sexual abuse is not about sex—it is about hate/violence and anger and selfishness. Named two perpetrators. S

#008M—My experience with 'men of God' practically ruined my life. The physical violence that came with my sexual abuse along with the "emotional abuse" can't be adequately described here. If not for the help of others in my teenage years, I would be dead today. S

#009M—I would appreciate any help in prosecuting/seeking restitution for harm done to me and my brother. The man is still a priest today, even though he abused my brother for over two years. S

#011F—I still feel shame. S

#012M—Named Priest is still in a parish. S

#016F—My life has been a living hell. I've been divorced twice. I've struggled to stay alive at times. I've spent 10+ years in therapy. I'm an over-achiever who is underemployed. I've struggled with _____, bulimia, and low self-esteem. On the plus side I am healing!! I have a deep relationship with God outside of the institutional church. But, I miss Mass and the Eucharist. I am not permitted to name the diocese due to a "gag" order. S

#017M—Lawsuit active in court system. S

#018F—Many people say that if someone was sexually abused as an adult, it is really hard to believe. And in my case, the perpetrator acted like "my boyfriend" at first. Asian countries are unlike western countries. If the clergy "sexually" abused someone, it would not be revealed in public. All covered up. Can't do anything. It's just awful and very sad. S

#019M—He was frequently moved to other parishes. Sent away for "treatment" at least four times. Finally, 30 years after he began to abuse kids, he was sent to prison for 275 years. S

#020F—I did not even get an apology with all of the church members that were informed. After four years, I have forgiven, but will never forget. I just hope he got the help he desperately needed. That's what I pray for. S

#021M—The Catholic hierarchy still doesn't get it about the issue of the Catholic clergy abusing the sheep. They have been lying and covering up for centuries. They actually believe each case is an isolated case when uncovered. And anyone who wants justice served is simply "trying to smear the RC church because he is possessed by the devil."

#022F—I am helping you with this survey but it has reopened a wound to do so! My motivation to let the diocese know after so many years was that he continued a friendship with my parents and told them I was at fault for hurting them when I "ran off" to the university. He was still trying to harm me after all these years. I told both of my parents and they cut off contact with him about 7 years ago. He took away my sense of safety and spiritual home. I still have difficulty going to church and do not trust clergy to be ministering to our family. 7 years ago, my husband and I both corresponded and met with the bishop's assistant. The priest denied it. My brother-in-law (attorney) and the Archdiocese of _____ Bishop talked with the_____officials. The Archdiocese's attorney met with my husband and me and my brother-in-law. The priest admitted to the charges but dismissed the importance. He gave no apology as requested by my husband. U

#023F—I was a big time victim. I hate the fucking Catholic Church with great passion!!! My whole life has been shit. May the fuckers rot in hell. S

#025M—If the Church had any sense, they would take a radical and hard line approach to investigating any rumors of allegations of sexual or other crimes perpetrated by priests. When any doubt occurs, the diocese should pursue the facts tenaciously and have little or no room for leniency. Measure ruined lives by souls saved. S

#026M—Fr. _____ was the priest offender. He was sent to a re-hab in _____. Moved on to _____. Committed suicide 2 years ago. _____ Archdiocese has gotten off scot-free. S

#027F—I wanted to become a nun. He was my advisor. S

#031M—Forgiveness is a powerful gift. Thank you. S

#032F—Although reporting was the toughest thing I've ever done, it's begun the healing. I needed to get my life—which has been one failure after another—back on track. The overall affect of the abuse has been two failed marriages, alcoholism and never sticking with or completing anything I started. Perhaps now. S

#033F—Thank you for the survey. I had more than one priest abuser and now I am ready to tell and not hide it anymore. I have found another survivor recently who had more than one priest abuser and he has gone public. Talking to him helped greatly. S

#034F—As a child, I told the high school counselor (a priest). His answer (after I told him who it was) was to say to me, "Well, at least you have good taste. Now, please leave." S

#035F—When I wanted information regarding counseling about this, I never knew the dysfunction it had done; not too many church people knew how to respond. I think this is so shocking that when even a church person gets the news of the shock, it sets in. Also the years for rebuilding and recovery is long. I also lost my marriage because of my husband not being sensitive to me. The whole horror of it colored my world so. I have learned that this issue is being addressed by the church which helps me a lot! S

#038F—Some of the questions were hard to answer because I remember abuse by at least five men, done as a group (sex ring). I've identified only two—I'm assuming they were all priests because the stuff occurred at the priests' lake cabins. My uncle and his friend had cabins next door to each other at a remote lake. (Uncle died and his friend was told that she was "not allowed to know what action was taken for the one still living.") S

#039F—As a young child, my brother was sexually assaulted by the parish priest in _____. This priest assaulted many young males who in turn, assaulted their classmates, both male and female. It created a warped environment. By the time I reached high school, I thought everything was based on power. I was a mess and ripe for assault myself. It took many years of therapy to get a clear picture of reality and I'm disgusted with the current behavior of the Roman Catholic Church in this area. S

#040F—I repressed the memories until I was 50 years old. I married a sexually abusive alcoholic. He divorced me after 15 years of marriage because I would not submit to his raping me when he was drunk. I always feared sex play and strange reactions to being touched sexually; I would break down and cry and I didn't understand why. I also have had several worsening episodes of severe depression and have been unable to hold a full-time job for 10 years. I have been in the care of a psychiatrist or psychologist for the past 25 years, and constantly over the last 5 years. I am in debt for medical bills over $12,000 and other bills because of low income. S

#041F—Many of this priest's victims came from families that the father of the family had died or the father was away often due to business. The families also relied on the church for support (spiritual and emotional support). S

#042M—His name is_____ and he basically was a counselor to me through high school. Then very shortly after graduation this episode happened. I felt too much shame to tell anyone (in 1959) and was afraid he'd lie and my family might not believe me over a priest (I know now that they would have believed me.) S

#043F—Thank you for this opportunity. S

#044F—Went for grief counseling. Had tried to contact bishop's office from the beginning 22 years ago but was always put off. Ex-priest friend contacted bishop and finally got me through in 1993–94. Child involved. Diocese secretly offered to pay off the child support settlement but at a decreased amount. Illegal, as case handled through superior court. Withdrawn quickly as a result. Have a 21-year-old daughter as a result of the rape by this priest. Have not seen her in three years due to the (priest/father) telling her I blackmailed him by serving him to pay back child support. When she turned 18, he bought her a car, helped her get an apartment and now sees her himself at least once a week. Scary since he's both a rapist and a pedophile. He had no interest, connection etc. with her till she turned 16 and counselor ordered him to become a responsible father. I have several letters of threat from the lawyer for this priest and the Diocese should I decide to go public. S

#045F—For the record, I do not think that celibacy is necessarily the cause of sexual abuse of minors. Many who perpetrate on children are, in fact, married. Look at what a problem incest is. Sexual abuse=abuse of power. The Catholic Church is plagued with a culture of secrecy and accompanying lack of accountability. This dynamic is more the problem than is celibacy, though certainly the psycho-sexual development of clergy needs to be examined. Priest recently received an award and is still in the system. S

#048F—This was difficult to do. I haven't thought of this for awhile now . . . forgot the priest had died, although I saved his obituary. S

#049F—The priest who abused me has never shown any remorse. He has admitted all but insists it was "consensual sex between two adults." The authorities of the church have not even smacked him on the hand. I would like to see him in prison. I am sure he damaged others. He cost me my faith and I have never been able to have sex with anyone else, so no husband, no children, etc. The priest is doing just fine. S

#050M—I had repressed memory of my sexual abuse for forty years. When I was fifty I had manifestations of post-traumatic stress disorder which I thought were job related (I was a firefighter in _____ for 28 years). I always had a feeling that something was wrong with me. In therapy, the secret was slowly exposed. I remained in therapy for ten years. Even today, when I see a priest raise the host and say "Body of Christ," I get so annoyed I want to get up and choke him. S

#056M—All children need to be protected. Later in life it haunts you. S

#058F—The jerk slipped something into my drink and almost got to penetration. I reported this associate pastor to the pastor. Jerk told pastor I lied. I got fired! I went to bishop . . . still, nothing done! All are still active in ministry. I don't practice religion and I am convinced _____ is_____ from case! U

#059M—Please poll priests who were sexually abused by priests when they were children. U

#061M—This report offered me for the first time, a chance to "publicly report" this abuse of power on me by the noted perpetrator. I do appreciate this opportunity. Feel free to call or correspond for any reason. Re legal: church said it did happen on church property. However, priest did "it" on his off time. No case. S

#062F—Criminal charges are still pending. This is since 1993. Civil action against the priest, diocese and parish are pending outcome of criminal process. My memories of the events did not return to me until 1992, though the events occurred in 1972. The diocese made a suggestion of an offer (no amount) in 1993. If you want more detailed info, let me know. I would be glad to disclose more. You can use my name. I now have a voice and should and need to use it. S

#063M—Clerical sexual abusers/predators should be laicized when their offense reaches the level of moral certitude in the eyes of the hierarchy. The lack of accountability by church authorities remains astounding. One wonders how many bishops/priests are co-opted by guilt and their own sexual histories from being interveners in these cases. S

#064M—Thank you for conducting this survey. S

#065M—Fr._____has long history of abuses. Believe his pimping me to vice squad was part of a coverup for him. Currently at _____ in _____. Public accusations came after me by others. _____ (religious order) have been covering therapy for last five years. S

#066M—There have been 6 priests publicly proven to be sexual abusers. The latest is Bishop _____. He is bishop to whom I reported Fr._____. S

#068M—Fr._____is a priest in _____ today, stayed on as the _____ for five more years. Bishop _____who later became the archbishop of_____ said he would transfer Fr. _____ and that he believed me and another student. He did not keep his word. Two other priests were also told about Fr._____. He was arrested for _____ in the early _____.

#069M—He was my Dad's best friend. I was named after him. (I was told the incident would be handled and to go away.) I will not go back to the Catholic religion. I have found another that has suited me quite well. I am surviving this abuse the best anyone can. It has taken me 15 years to get my life back together as this abuse destroyed my mind as well as my spirit. The priest that abused me will see no jail time and not be punished for what he did to me because the Catholic Church sheltered and protected him. I think the Catholic Church should clean their fucking house!!! S

#071M—At the time I reported, priest was reported by other victim—transferred to an all boys' school. Although I think "mandatory celibacy" is an idea well past its time, I also think the Catholic Church should put more emphasis on the victims than on the offenders; show compassion; provide psychological and spiritual counseling; contact outside authorities (law) and provide evidence in a timely manner; strip offender of priestly duties. Do all of the above first sincerely, and then worry about "mandatory celibacy." Married men can also be sexually abusive. Feel free to contact me if you need further information. S

#074M—I cannot in good conscience be bonded with a church which still supports the molestation of children. I have had years of therapy but am stuck waiting for the church to "show" it is sorry for what happened. This could be shown if it stopped the cover up and denial to protect its assets. S

#075F—I developed disassociative disorder to handle the abuse of my biological father. The priest was told about the incest when my father died. He began sexual abuse within three months. The memories were repressed for over 20 years. When I learned of the abuse, I filed a lawsuit and diocese used statute of limitations to avoid the truth. S

#077F—I was a student in his (college) class. He said he was a therapist and offered to help anyone who was troubled. At the time the abuse occurred, I was in a desperate state of despondency due to sexual orientation and gender issues that I was unable to resolve despite numerous attempts to seek psychiatric and therapeutic help during earlier adolescence. I feel there's unfinished business because my perpetrator has not made appropriate amends. I don't trust professionals (lawyers, therapists, etc). They did offer to pay for some therapy but when I thought about it, I realized that's not what I really want or need. A just financial settlement would be in order. I am in the process of writing a full report of my abuse. S

#079F—This perpetrator also sexually physically abused two male children. U

#080M—He still has his outfits, since dismissed still dresses as a priest, is under probation court supervision. Part of the "BYOB" club "bring your own boy" for recruiting men into priesthood. U

#081F—I requested a very modest cash amount (a percentage of my therapy costs). At first, my requests were ignored. I sought advice from a bishop (totally uninvolved with the case) who contacted the provincial on my behalf. Provincial sent letter of apology on behalf of the order and check (as requested) after conferring with my therapist. S

#082F—Arrested sexual development in the area of sexual orientation. I filled this out but would describe my experience as one of sexual exploitation more than abuse. Some of the time the sexualized behavior was not unwanted—only inappropriate. It was the most confusing time of my life and it has taken years to make any sense of it. I do not believe that clergy sexual abuse would end with an end to celibacy as a prerequisite to ordination. Much more complicated. S

#084M—I was punished instead of the priest. My abuse was extremely ritualistic both in form and intent. I believe others, including family members, were also abused but have no proof. I believe my perp was a member of a ring or coven. When I disclosed the abuse to another priest in confession, I was hauled out and made to apologize to the perp. The perp than requested transfer to another parish on his own. S

#085F—Fr. _____ propositioned me twice. His superiors ignored me then denied it. Finally, I was blamed. He was emotionally fixated at age 14 when he entered religious life. S

#086F—The Catholic Church is looking to get off the hook financially—from compensating those it has ruined for life. I detest it like I do cancer. It has caused spiritual annihilation for many. The hierarchs are all a bunch of pompous assholes looking to stomp us out like bugs. I'll die hating them all. S

#087F—My father "set me up" when I was very young. I was very lonely growing up in an alcoholic home. (Father was alcoholic.) Brother_____ was my "friend" until I realized that this was wrong. It was so long ago, details are foggy and repression has taken away much of it. S

#088F—A priest during my childhood caused me to feel guilty of sin about my incest. This same priest from my childhood did not sexually abuse, but he was sexually abusive to my younger sister, cousin and other young girls by requesting them to do self masturbation in the confessional and then tell him how it felt—probably for his own sexual pleasure. This was never reported in his lifetime. No action taken; some parishioners believed me; others did not. Bishop had priest apologize to me. S

#089M—Legal action was taken against diocese after they stopped paying for my personal therapy. This not by coincidence occurred once the statute to take civil action in the state of _____ ran out. It was at that time that I took civil action and the church re-abused me—putting me through a string of depositions to see if they could wear me down. That did not work! **Get the word out!** S

#090F—I also proceeded to file a complaint with the marriage and family therapists Assn of America. Resulted in 1 year probation (for priest); and the State Board Licensing for Marriage and Family Therapists, to which this priest had made application. Trial was held in Administrative Court in _____ and the licensure was denied. A 22-page report was promulgated by the Administrative judge and I will make that available. The transcript of the trial is available under the _____Open Records Act to anyone who requests it. S

#091M—Your last three questions assume that the abused knew what sexual abuse is. As a child, I had no idea what was going on. You also have no questions on recovery from the abuse and how the Catholic Community abuses you all over again if you come forward. S

#094F—Thank you for letting me participate in this survey. U

#096M—Since reporting six years ago, diocese has side-stepped issues and now with court case pending, wants me to lie and deny facts. S

#097M—All four of these priests surprised me. I immediately set them straight and that was that. S

#100F—I was raped, sodomized, cut, burned, beaten, hung and forced to participate in "rituals." The priests taught me they were sent by God to save me from my sins. I completely repressed the memories for over 35 years. The memories came back when as a teacher in our parish school, I caught a priest molesting a little girl. Even though there were other witnesses, the priest just keeps getting moved from parish to parish. I hope if I just speak out maybe it will stop. S

#102M—Don't know what more to say except that the more I heal the more I discover the wreckage done to my life. I've come so close to suicide so many times, and about a month ago, I was really close. Really a huge job recovering and yet gets better daily (the more) I do the work. THANKS A LOT! S

#106M—My parents continued in therapy (I did not) for 10 years when the school decided to stop payment. We found an attorney who was handling another student in the same school. The attorney fought on our behalf. After 10 years there was a $75,000 settlement with order not to speak-attached! School was most cooperative in paying all bills for 10 years. Once approached by an attorney school settled within 9 months, fearing publicity. There was never admission of guilt. U

#107M—Hooray for this survey! The 3-year experience I went through with this priest was the main reason I did not stay in the seminary in 1971–72. I would have been a damn good priest had this not happened. I sometimes often wonder how many others went through the same hell. I truly look forward to the results of the study! Bless you one and all. S

#108F—My children, 3 out of 4, were also molested by a priest when they were ages 6–11 & 12. The priest plead guilty and received a sentence of 7 years probation. This occurred in the _____ diocese in 1979–1983. I went for counseling to my employer/pastor who made advances to me and I was vulnerable and in need of emotional/spiritual support. This was a 5-year sexual relationship which finally ended in 1989. Since then, I've obtained my graduate degree in psychology and understand this relationship was sexual abuse. As an MFCC, I would lose my license if I did what the priest did to me. S

#109F—Fr. _____ (uncle and pervert) raped me the first time at 5 yrs old, the last time at 13. I told a nun at 15 and she took me under her wing and into her bed. At age 38, I went to a lawyer who told me nothing could be done because he was dead and a relative. If this is not accurate, please advise me differently. Thank you. S

#112F—Because I reported this matter and subsequently filed a federal lawsuit, I would find it difficult to gain employment in my field (career consultant/HS generalist) I also feel that I am unwelcome in the diocese whereas the perpetrator simply moved to a new assignment and has been permitted to continue his ministry—as a welcome member of the "clergy." The only priests who supported me (and many knew the truth) were also chastised by the bishop and other church officials. S

#115M—Although the priest admitted his sexual offenses, the diocese admitted knowing of his offense and transferred him 15 times in 15 years. In 1997, the _____ Supreme Court ruled a church could NOT be held responsible. Victims in 20 other U.S. States can hold churches legally responsible and do receive financial settlements. This is unfair. S

#117M—I never reported what happened as "abuse" because I always thought that meant physical contact. However, there are other forms of abuse, including coercion of behavior buying influence and the teaching of sexual dysfunction to impressionable teenagers which broadly come under how you describe "sexual abuse." This actually continued into my adult life, and resulted in such severe harassment that I had to resign my job and emigrate to the U.S. (from Ireland). S

#118F—[Cable TV] made a movie of his _____ which he was doing at the same time he was abusing me! Met in 9/62, sexual abuse did not start until 1963. Long grooming period. Heavy smoker and alcoholic. Had alcohol treatment in '66. Now works in chemical dependency field. Very attached to his mother. Non-involved father. S

#119M—I am 65 years old now. I never told anybody I was in a mental hospital at 18. I was lost for 10–15 years. I can't blame it all on these experiences. I am retired now—had a good marriage and job in city of _____ last 25 years. I was 12 going away from home to seminary—hawk waiting for me—had my pants down the first month. S

#120M—When I received the questionnaire, I thought it better not to reply as it would bring up bad memories (76 years old). I was ill in the infirmary and the brother in charge, the Infirmarian, came up to my bed and fondled me. This lasted about 1 or 2 minutes, and I was frightened to death. I did not know how to mention it to anyone. What has bothered me since then is that it could have been happening to many other young persons who would be sent to the infirmary in his care . . . I might have prevented others . . . I was only a child. Many times in my years between 12 and maybe 19, I would have nightmares that I was still living in that place and I would awaken frightened. Thank you for your efforts in your studies on this problem. S

#121M—In November 1995, a front page article about my abuse appeared in my hometown paper . . . it was a very important part of my recovery. S

#122F—Thank you for simply asking! It's rare that someone wants to hear this. S

#124F—Thank you for the work you have done to assist in support and reporting. My history has serious traumas as a child. I have received therapy, have reported the priest abuse without legally proceeding. The religious order has not responded appropriately or responsibly. Those in administration are friends who were terribly afraid and unethical. I have never been intimidated by their inability to proceed. They are typical and that is so concerning since many reports must be ignored. The priest who abused me died after he read years of reports that I sent to him. It's not over. I will continue to confront them. S

#129M—There were questions about his character as far back as 1971. His ordination was refused at that time. Complaints started in 1975, two years after he was ordained. He was transferred to my church in 1980 amid accusations of sexual misconduct/abuse. All records of those complaints disappeared from the sheriff's office somehow. Of course, the diocese denied any wrong-doing or cover-up. S

#130F—Mandatory celibacy—ridiculous—should be optional and in seminary they should be put through a battery of psychological tests—the healthy Roman priests are those who left to go into ministry in other churches because they chose to marry. Thank you for doing this study. I hope you will be instrumental in helping to make a change. Two men (priests) here in _____ diocese who are known to me to be pedophiles—are moved from parish to parish— and are given access to small children. Another has been accused by church secretary in local parish of molesting her. She was the wife of the parish (_____) deacon who was told by Bishop _____ that he would be removed as deacon and laicized if they told. This clergy abuse has had devastating effects on mind, body and spirit. I owe my life to my husband who has been and continues to be supportive, my many doctors and therapist! S

Center for the Study of Religious Issues
P.O. Box 2473
CSRI Framingham, MA 01703–2473
Email: <u>CSRI99@aol.com</u>

June, 1999

We are conducting a series of studies regarding mandatory celibacy in the Roman Catholic Priesthood, as well as clergy sexual abuse. This particular questionnaire is to establish certain general demographics in relation to victims of sexual abuse by Roman Catholic priests. What we mean by "sexual abuse" in this survey is: any unwanted sexual experience, such as emotional abuse of a sexual nature, sexual harassment, inappropriate exposure and/or unwanted touching experiences ranging from fondling to penetration.

We hope you will be willing to assist in this study by responding to each of the following confidential questions, aggregate results of which will be used as part of a general statistical report. Some of the questions will apply to you; others will ask your opinion about the priest offender.

Please return the confidential questionnaire in the prepaid self-addressed envelope provided. Do not sign the questionnaire unless you wish to receive a copy of the results. *If you were **not** abused by a Roman Catholic priest, please return the questionnaire in the stamped self-addressed envelope provided.*

We would like to thank you for your participation in this sociological project, which may be beneficial to other scientific researchers in the future. **CSRI** is an independent research organization and is not affiliated with any religious community.

Louise J. Haggett
Research Coordinator

Questionnaire

General Instructions: Please place a check mark on the line to the left of your choice of answer, or write in an answer where appropriate.

Part One

The following questions are to establish general information about respondents.

What is your gender?

1. _____ A. Male
   _____ B. Female

2. What is your age? _____

3. What is your birth year? _____

4. What is your highest level of education?
   _____ A. No formal education
   _____ B. Grade school only
   _____ C. Some high school
   D. High School (or
   _____   equivalent)diploma
   _____ E. Vocational training
   F. High School plus
   _____   vocational training
   _____ G. Some college
   _____ H. College degree
   _____ I. Graduate work
   _____ J. Graduate degree

5. Are you still in school?
   _____ A. Yes
   _____ B. What level?
   _____ c. No

6. If you are in the workplace, what type of work do you do today?

   _____

   _____

7. How often do you attend Mass at a Roman Catholic Church?
   _____ A. Never or hardly ever
   _____ B. 1–3 times per year
   _____ C. 3–11 times per year
   _____ D. 1–3 times per month
   _____ E. 1–3 times per week
   _____ F. I am not Catholic
   _____ G. I am Catholic but attend services at another church
   _____ H. I was raised Catholic but do not participate in any Catholic Church activity

If you are not Catholic, you may skip to Question 9

8. If you are Catholic, did you attend Mass as a child?
   _____ A. Never or hardly ever
   _____ B. 1–3 times per year
   _____ C. 3–11 times per year
   _____ D. 1–3 times per month
   _____ E. 1–3 times per week
   _____ F. I am Catholic but attended services at another church
   _____ G. I was raised Catholic but did not participate in any Roman Catholic church-related activities

Part Two

The following questions are about an unwanted sexual experience (henceforth referred to as "sexual abuse") which you have had. For purposes of this study, "Unwanted sexual experience"(sexual abuse) includes emotional abuse of a sexual nature, sexual harassment, inappropriate exposure and/or unwanted touching experiences ranging from fondling to penetration.

9. Were you sexually abused by a Roman Catholic priest?
   (see above description)
   _____ A. Yes
   _____ B. No

If the answer is no, please STOP HERE. This survey is only for victims of sexual abuse by Roman Catholic clergy. Thank you.

9a. The sexual abuse included:
   _____ A. No physical contact
   _____ B. Some physical contact
   _____ C. Primarily physical contact
   _____ D. Both physical and non-physical offenses

10. How was the priest offender known to you?
   _____ A. A relative of the family
   _____ B. A friend of the family
   _____ C. Casual acquaintance
   _____ D. Stranger (someone previously unknown to me)
   _____ E. Other *(please specify)*

11. At what age did this sexual abuse begin?
   _____ A. 0–6 years old
   _____ B. 7–9 years old
   _____ C. 10–13 years old
   _____ D. 14–15 years old
   _____ E. 16–18 years old
   _____ F. 19 years old
   _____ G. 20+ years old

12. At what age did this sexual abuse end?
   _____ A. 0–6 years old
   _____ B. 7–9 years old
   _____ C. 10–13 years old
   _____ D. 14–15 years old
   _____ E. 16–18 years old
   _____ F. 19 years old
   _____ G. 20+ years old
   (see next page)

13. How long did it last?
   _____ A. One time only
   _____ B. 1 week to 1 month
   _____ C. 2–6 months
   _____ D. 7 months–1 year
   _____ E. 1–4 years
   _____ F. 5–7 years
   _____ G. 8–10 years
   _____ H. Over 10 year

14. Do you know the approximate age of the **priest offender** at the time you were sexually abused?
   _____ A. 20–29 years old
   _____ B. 30–39 years old
   _____ C. 40–49 years old
   _____ D. 50+ years old
   _____ E. Don't know

15. Do you know if the priest
    offender sexually abused others?
    _____ A. Yes
    _____ B. No
    _____ C. Don't know

*If the answer to Question 15 is
"Yes," please go on to Question 16.
If the answer to Question 15 is "No"
or "Don't Know," please go on to
Question 17.*

16. If yes, how many other
    victims are you personally
    aware of?
    _____ A. 2–3 other victims
    _____ B. 4–6 other victims
    _____ C. 7–10 other victims
    _____ D. 11–20 other
            victims
    _____ E. 21–40 other
            victims
    _____ F. 40+ or more
            victims

17. Do you know how long he
    had been a priest at the time
    he first sexually abused you?
    _____ A. 0–8 years
    _____ B. 9–13 years
    _____ C. 14–20 years
    _____ D. 21–30 years
            (see next column)
    _____ E. 31–40 years
    _____ F. 41+ years
    _____ G. Don't know

18. How did you become
    acquainted?
    (please check all that apply)
    _____ A. I attended
            parochial school
    _____ B. I was an altar
            server
    _____ C. I attended CCD/
            CYO/other
            religious/social
            organization
    _____ D. I was a church
            employee
    _____ E. I was a church
            volunteer
    _____ E. I came for
            counseling
    _____ G. Other *(please
            specify)*
    _____

19. When was your abuse
    reported?
    _____ A. Never
    _____ B. At the time it
            happened
    _____ C. Within 6 months
            of the offense
    _____ D. 7 months to
            2 years
    _____ E. 3–10 years
    _____ F. 11–20 years
    _____ G. 20+ years _____

If "never," skip to Question 24.

20. To whom was it reported?
    (check all that apply)
    _____ A. Pastor
    _____ B. Another priest
    _____ C. Bishop
    _____ D. Other church
    official *(please specify)*

    _____

    _____ E. Legal authorities
    (e.g. police)
    _____ F. Professionals
    (e.g., counselor)
    _____ G. Parents or
    guardians
    _____ H. Other *(please
    specify)*

    _____

21. Discipline action taken *(check
    all that apply)*
    _____ A. Treatment center
    _____ B. Jail time (how
    long?)

    _____

    _____ C. Priest sent to a
    different parish
    (see next page)
    _____ D. Priest was
    dismissed from
    all clerical functions
    _____ E. Other *(please
    specify)*

    _____

    _____ F. Don't know

22. The primary reason
    disciplinary action was
    taken related to
    _____ A. Parties were
    convinced by
    evidence of the
    offense

_____ B. Public attention
was drawn to the
offense
_____ C. Other *(please
specify)*

_____

23. Were you offered and/or given
    a financial settlement in the
    matter of the abuse?
    _____ A. Yes
    _____ B. Yes, but the details
    must remain private
    _____ C. No
    _____ D. Other (please
    specify)

    _____

24. Is the priest offender still in
    active ministry today?
    _____ A. Yes
    _____ B. No
    _____ C. Don't know

25. How would you describe the
    needs of the offending priest?
    _____ A. Biological (e.g.,
    natural sexual
    need)
    _____ B. Emotional
    (e.g., loneliness)
    _____ C. Authoritarian
    personality (abuse
    of power)
    _____ D. Other (please
    specify)

    _____

    _____ E. Don't know

26. In which diocese did the
    sexual abuse take place?

    _____

27. Were you sexually abused before or since by another perpetrator?

_____ A. Yes

_____ 1. By how many *before?*

_____ 2. By how many *since?*

_____ B. No

If the answer is Yes, please respond to the following questions. If the answer is No, please stop here and thank you for completing this survey. You may leave any comments you wish in the space provided.

28. Was the offender:

_____ A. Male?

_____ B. Female?

29. Was the offender:

_____ A. A Roman Catholic priest?

_____ B. A minister of another faith?

_____ C. Teacher, coach, scout leader, professional counselor, etc.?

_____ D. Other (please specify)?

_____

Thank you. Any comments you make will be kept in strict confidence and be used only as part of a general report

Comments: _____

_____

_____

_____

_____

_____

_____

_____

_____

_____

Please send me a copy of the study results.

Name _____

Address _____

City_____ State_____ Zip_____

(Your name will remain confidential)

6

Literary Study—Loneliness

I n social research, it is difficult if not impossible to prove cause and effect in phenomena. According to Earl Babbie, author of the textbook, *The Practice of Social Research* (1995), "The first requirement in a causal relationship between two variables is that the cause must precede the effect in time. The second requirement is that the two variables must be empirically correlated with one another (testability as opposed to groundless speculation), and the third requirement is that the observed empirical correlation between two variables cannot be explained away as being due to the influence of some third variable that causes both of them" (70). Babbie goes on to explain "necessary" and "sufficient" causes, conditions that must be present for the effect to follow or that will guarantee the effect (71).

The studies presented in this book are introduced together because of correlations that were *not* found until the reports were combined in the fall of 2003, unexpected relationships that might not have been discovered otherwise. We believe that this may also be the reason the following discussion and conclusion has eluded the scientific community and others curious about the genesis of clergy sexual abuse, until now.

Clergy sexual abuse *is* different from and more complex than abuse that takes place in other segments of the society. Mandatory celibacy is equally a complex issue. When combined, however, the two can create a pathological phenomenon. For years, and more recently in an HBO TV special regarding Celibacy (2004), those connected with the Catholic Church have said that "mandatory celibacy does not cause clergy sexual abuse." True, not all celibate priests are sexual perpetrators. However, when mandatory celibacy is imposed on certain individuals, it may lead to clergy sexual abuse. In this, we theorize "cause and effect." Our demographic profile in especially the adolescent Victim Study in chapter 3 indicate that, with the exception of the few serial perpetrators with multiple victims, the majority of clergy perpetrators differ from a typical sexual perpetrator among the general population. Our reasoning follows.

Loneliness and the Celibate Priesthood

Our first clue that intense loneliness might be a major aspect beyond a "latent variable" of the chain reaction that may lead to clergy sexual abuse began when almost 60 percent of the respondents in the Haggett reassessment of the Priest Study (chapter 1) wrote in "loneliness," "lack of intimacy," and wanting "marriage and family" as reasons that priests break their vows. More telling, however, were the responses from the victims of clergy sexual abuse who were asked what they thought were the needs of the priest(s) who abused them. That almost 40 percent of the victims/survivors who are as angry as they are that priests stole their innocence and maimed them psychologically for life would even consider or admit in retrospect that priests might be lonely is an astounding finding. In fact, over 50 percent of the victims retrospectively indicated biological and emotional needs, defined as "sex" and "loneliness," respectively, on the victim survey instrument as part of their response. When this information was combined with the overwhelming comments about loneliness from the priest respondents that were freely made and not suggested by the authors of the study, it was apparent that the issue of loneliness among priests needed to be investigated further.

Loneliness Studies in the Priesthood

Several studies have been conducted and many books and articles have been written about the celibate priesthood over the years, some by priests themselves. In discussing mandatory celibacy, one major side effect has been consistently mentioned throughout—*loneliness*. Here are a few examples:

- The First Five Years of the Priesthood (Dean R. Hoge 2002). This was a quantitative study of priests during their first five years after ordination, including those who left within five years. Quotes:
  - "Our study was suffused with talk about celibacy, loneliness, desire for intimacy and homosexuality—more so than expected. Much of this is not new but the frank talk about homosexuality is something new" (102).
  - "Among priests who resigned their clerical ministry, the only thing in common in the four sets of reasons for leaving was *loneliness*" (63).
  - An article within *Five Years* written by the late Rev. James Gill listed 13 stresses that priests have. Number one was "loneliness" (117).

- *Goodbye Father* (Schoenherr and Yamane 2002). "Young priests who endorse modern values, who find *loneliness* a problem, and who prefer marriage over celibacy will more likely resign" (21).
- *Full Pews and Empty Altars. Demographics of the Priest Shortage in the U.S. Catholic Dioceses* (Schoenherr and Young 1993). This study was based on data about priests leaving clerical ministry that was obtained from diocesan files in the early 1980s. Schoenherr and Young wrote, "Poor retention has been a persistent problem for the entire 25-year period following the Second Vatican Council. All the

studies conclude that the major reasons why young priests resign are adherence to modern values and problems with *loneliness* and celibacy" (335).

- *Shattered Vows: Priests Who Leave* (Rice 1990) "From an editorial in the *Catholic Herald*, London: 8 May 1987: 'What is clear is that a blind eye is being turned to the large, indeed increasing, amount of unhappy priests and the very high incidence of homosexuality and drunkenness among clergy due, ultimately, to *loneliness*'" (159).

- *The Changing Face of the Priesthood* (Cozzens 2000). Cozzens served as vicar in a large midwestern diocese: "Among priests who came to [him] to announce leaving, few expressed anger at Church, pastor or of unforgiving parishioners. Not one mentioned loss of faith . . . many did, however, speak of *loneliness* and a desire for intimacy" (25).

- *NORC.* "NORC [National Opinion Research Center] found resignations more frequent among young priests who found *loneliness* a personal problem" (Schoenherr and Young 1993:222).

- *A Secret World: Sexuality and the Search for Celibacy*—a study of 1,500 priests (Sipe 1990). "The depth of the aloneness that must be embraced to support celibacy cannot be minimized" (63). "'*Lonely*' is one of the most frequent replies when one asks a celibate how he feels" (260). "*The person who cannot tolerate true aloneness cannot move beyond this level of celibacy and therefore remains vulnerable to sexual compromises even after years of discipline*" (261).

- *Celibacy in Crisis* (Sipe 2003). "There is no way to practice and achieve celibacy other than by penetrating the aloneness, not merely sustaining it" (39). "For Priests in for 22–27 years, it is lack of companionship rather than sexual discharge that threaten the celibate commitment" (298).

- First-person account: Sean Connolly: "Sundays were the worst. You did all the Masses. All the Baptisms. After Mass, I'd sit on the wall by the Church, and speak to the few people going by. I used to envy the local priests—they could go home to Ma on Sunday. I used to sit on that wall outside St. Cecilia's; the intensity and the pain of it—feeling I don't belong to anyone here" (Rice 1990:34).

- When asked about loneliness, Milwaukee's Archbishop Rembert Weakland told *The New Yorker* in 1991:

> *Loneliness is an easy way of talking about it. It really comes down to celibacy, don't you think? The trick in dealing with celibacy is to understand that there is no true substitute for the intimacy of marriage. We were taught that the Divine Office, your community, your prayer life were substitutes, but they are not. Travel, an intellectual life, and in the case of a bishop, a measure of authority, power: these are not substitutes, either. I'm over sixty—for me it's not about sex. When it hits me hardest is not when I'm in trouble or want to pour my heart out because I'm depressed. It's when I have a great idea that I'd like to share with someone, when I've heard a new piece of music and want someone to sit down and listen with me. My trip to Russia last summer (1990): I have no one—nobody on the same wave length—with whom I can talk about what I saw, what I felt. That's a burden I have to live with. While I see the great merit in celibacy—the freedom it gives you—perhaps there are people who can't make that sacrifice. And yet we con-tinue to demand that they do—if they want to be priests. Across-the-board celibacy works to our detriment as a Church . . . Men who leave the priesthood because of loneliness are not weak. They are simply good men who have fallen in love with good women. (Wilkes:53)*

Not all celibate priests are lonely, and not all celibate priests are sexual perpetrators. No research has ever been conducted, however, that compares these two variables, measuring them against the general population; furthermore, no separate research that has been conducted on either subject has ever combined findings from a causal aspect. The inclusion of loneliness in a cause equation as part of a chain reaction, therefore, is an original finding. One of the reasons it may not have been considered in the causal factors is that for the hierarchy or for a priest—a male—to admit intense loneliness would be to admit weakness[1] among a subgroup whose persona projects authority and spiritual strength. The idea of being weak makes the priest fallible in a culture that has idealized him as a divine being and puts him on a pedestal with other Catholic icons such as Jesus and the Blessed Virgin Mary. This is a difficult role to play.

Loneliness Studies in General

Our next step was to investigate what can happen to individuals who suffer from intense loneliness. Research clearly demonstrates that persistent intense loneliness has strong correlations with low self-esteem (in some instances, high self-esteem leading to an authoritative nature), substance abuse, suicide, and crime (Rokach 2001, 2000b, 1990, Kim 1997, Nurmi et al. 1997, Jones and Carver 1991, in Nurmi et al. ibid, Jones 1982, Weiss 1982, Russell 1982, Brennan 1982) and that an absence of a mate produces even greater loneliness: sadness, depression, boredom, self-pity, longing to be with one special person (Rubinstein and Shaver, 1980:211).

"Loneliness is multidimensional and greater loneliness has been associated with higher levels of mental health difficulties, the use of more passive emotion-focused coping to deal with stress, greater social skills inadequacies, lower self-esteem, less interpersonal trust, less liking for people, greater intimacy deficits and less satisfaction with life" (DiTommaso, Brannen and Best 2004:116). Studies conducted by Weiss (1973), Jones, Hansson and Smith (1980), Hill, Rubin and Peplau (1976), Russell, Peplau and Cutrona (1980), and Peplau and Perlman (1982) have also indicated greater loneliness among interpersonal relational status and dating several people ver-

---

[1] As previously reported, 16.9 percent of priests wrote in "weakness" as a factor breaking their vows in the Priest Study (chapter 1).

sus someone special because of lack of romantic involvement and intimate friends.

In contrast to stereotype, however, the elderly do not generally report a high degree of loneliness unless they are physically and financially unable to maintain contact with others. "While a grieving survivor in a spousal relationship where mortality takes place, this [loneliness] is not considered a psychiatric disorder. A possible explanation is that the elderly have learned to adjust to solitude, or may prefer it" (West, Kellner and Moore-West 1986:353). Sociologist and feminist Gloria Steinem aptly put it in an interview when asked about the mourning of her husband's death in 2003: "In depression, nothing matters." In sadness and grief, "everything matters. Everything was more poignant" (Kornblum 2005:1D).

Researchers also agree that "Voluntary solitude is not synonymous with loneliness. Lonely people do not voluntarily enter into that emotional state; rather they 'find themselves' feeling sometimes desperately lonely for reasons even they may not fully understand. Neither is being 'alone' synonymous with loneliness" (Booth 2000). According to Booth, "Loneliness is fundamentally debilitating, it is appropriate for both clinicians and researchers to attempt to understand it, both as a condition in itself and as it relates to other conditions . . . accompanied by dysfunctional and sometimes life-threatening correlates . . . sometimes masked by or mistaken for . . . depression" (1). "It may well be that simply having people in our lives is insufficient; perhaps they need to be persons whom we perceive to be able to satisfy our needs for close, intimate contact" (3). Booth links loneliness to stress and the immune system, as well as psychiatric dysfunctions such as narcissism, suicide, depression, anxiety, alcoholism, dependency, and hypochondriasis.

Booth wrote that "the longer people suffer from (loneliness), the more vulnerable they become to both physical and psychological risk factors. Loneliness warrants consideration as a potentially serious dysfunction. This is perhaps even truer when we examine the relationship between loneliness and depression. Not all lonely people are depressed, nor are all depressed people lonely, but the two conditions share significant variance in many of the studies that have measured them both" (6).

To these studies, we add, "Single adult men are the loneliest among older folks; being unattached—no spouse, no sexual partner . . ." (West et al. 1986:353).

While there is little or no research on the side effects of intense loneliness among priests, there is mention of such issues relating to substance abuse, depression, and suicide in books by Sipe (1990) and Hoge (2002).

Loneliness and Substance Abuse

In a literary study on loneliness and alcohol abuse, researcher Ingemar Akerlind's findings indicated that "the use of alcohol as an effort to establish contact and cope with loneliness is widely recognized and sometimes regarded as a gateway to drinking problems" (1992:405). "There are clues in the research that loneliness may lead to alcoholism, drug abuse and other behavioral disorders. The causal pathways are, however, still not clear. Abuse may not only represent an attempt to alleviate the pain connected with loneliness but it may also be a means of getting in touch with other people or coping with social society" (Rook in Akerlind 1992:411). Many victims have told stories of being induced with alcohol and other substances as part of their abuse by their clergy perpetrators. "Loneliness does play a significant role in the life of an alcoholic, more so than in many of the other groups combined" (Medora and Woodward 1991:776).

The Priest Study in chapter 2 had a 6.8 percent write-in response of substance abuse as a reason for breaking vows.

Loneliness and Self-Esteem

Low self-esteem or lack of self-actualization is the major personality disposition most associated with loneliness (DiTommaso et al. 2004, Booth 2000, Jones and Carver in Nurmi et al. ibid., Medora and Woodward 1991, Peplau and Perlman 1982). According to James Dietch (1978), "The involvement in a love relationship is associated with the attainment of high levels of self-actualization (self-esteem)" (632). This would be consistent with the Gratification Theory coined by behavioral scientist Abraham Maslow, in which he lists as the first level of basic needs necessary for an individual to reach self-actualization: food, water, sleep, and sex. (Maslow 1954:16). According to Maslow, "Higher needs will not even appear in consciousness until lower, pre-potent needs are gratified" (41). One regression in a hierarchy of needs study found "the lower the participants' self-esteem, the more they reported feelings of loneliness" (Nurmi et al. 1997:770).

Baumiester, Smart and Boden (1999) presented a different side of self-esteem based on an interdisciplinary review of evidence about aggression. "In most cases, the perpetrators appear to be men who privately believe in their own superior worth, but who encounter others who impugn or dispute that belief. Violence may be especially likely when the individual lacks alternative means to prove or establish his superiority" (257). Baumiester et al. also ask, "Might high self-esteem be a false veneer to cover up low self-esteem?" (272). Another study on loneliness indicated that "men who are likely involved in striving for accomplishments may not have the time or inclination to reflect much about any loneliness they may experience" (Coon 1992, in Rokach, 2000:81). Still another study on self-esteem and criminal behavior patterns concluded that "respondents who perceived themselves as criminal and bad seemed to identify to a greater degree with the criminal structure and scored high on the self-esteem scale" (Arnold 1980:107).

In addition to "loneliness," our data in the Victim Study revealed a relatively high percentage of respondents who attributed their abuse to authoritarian priests . . . and abuse of power. This finding opens new doors for future research.

Loneliness and Suicide

Suicidal tendencies as a reaction to persistent intense loneliness was mentioned by several of the above loneliness researchers. Emil Durkheim, who introduced "suicide" as a social theory in 1897, said, "When individuals are over-regulated by norms, beliefs and values in their social relations and when they have no individual freedom discretion or autonomy, they are potential victims of fatalistic [sic] suicide" (Durkheim in Turner et al. 1995:332). A 1997 literature review on intense loneliness by Michael Loos quoted, "Persistent loneliness may jeopardize an individual's psychological well-being and increase risk of suicide" (Loos in Kim 1997:591). The same review also produced the following from Hackney and Wrenn (1990), "The growing problem of loneliness is manifested in several indicators including addictions, suicide, depression and criminal behavior (Loos 2002:203).

There have been reports of priest suicides for several years relating to clergy sexual abuse. In 1992, a letter was received by this author from a Kentucky priest who was leaving to marry. He wrote, "The same week I left, another priest here took his life and another was publicly accused of sexual abuse. Just yesterday, another pastor left his ministry and another was asked by his parish council to leave."

In 1994, priest psychologist Stephen Rossetti wrote, "We are aghast when a priest ends his life and wonder how he could do it. Considering the circumstances, I am surprised that more do not. It is difficult to remain in this world as a 'living disgrace . . . the list is growing'" (8). As of August 2002 the published count for priest suicides was 16 (CBSNews online 2002).

Loneliness and Crime

Several researchers mentioned crime emanating from persistent intense loneliness: "Addictive behavior (alcohol and drug abuse), suicide and crime 'instead of' self-search and a friendly reaching out, they engaged in behavior that was immoral, socially unacceptable and often destructive" (Rokach 1990:48). "Loneliness contributes to criminality and recidivism" (Rokach and Koledin 1997:168). Rokach recommended that "clinicians, especially those who work with criminals, gain a better understanding not only of how lonely their patients are, but also the 'flavour' of their experience, its meanings and various manifestations for therapeutic purposes" (169). Booth said, "Many problems exist for lonely people that lead to preoccupation with their loneliness and a behavioral repertoire that is counterproductive in terms of ameliorating (improving) their own condition" (6).

In *The Psychology of Criminal Conduct*, Andrews and Bonta (1994) wrote, "It is not anger, hate, the search for adventure or even too much ambition (greed) that causes criminal activity. Rather, criminal behavior reflects awareness of limited opportunity and feelings of alienation, isolation, powerlessness, normlessness and personal distress" (97).

One study of the negative implications of loneliness saw alienation and lack of intimacy as critical in the development of criminality in general and sexual offending in particular" (Marshall 1989, in Rokach 2001:278). "Most sexual offenders commit offenses for motives other than purely sexual" (Schneider 1997:320). In a study on the psychological profiles of child sex offenders in Ireland and using Marshall's theory, Marsa et al. wrote that "insecure adult attachment styles compromise sex offenders' capacity to make and maintain satisfying intimate relationships and so lead to loneliness" (Marsa,et al. 2004:246). "Logic and clinical experience have resulted in a widespread assumption that loneliness is likely in patients with various psychiatric problems: depression, anxiety, personality disorders, schizophrenia, alcoholism, bulimia and child abuse" (West et al. 1986:354).

American Psychiatric Association

The American Psychiatric Association's (APA) third edition of their manual, *Diagnostic and Statistical Manual of Mental Disorders* (DSM-III-R) included "intense loneliness" as a "differential diagnosis" under the heading "Pedophilia" (285). The "differential diagnosis" designation was eliminated in the next edition, DSM-IV as well as future editions.

The intent of Richard Booth's paper on loneliness (2000) was to strongly recommend that the APA consider "loneliness" as a psychological disorder. Booth challenged the APA "to determine whether loneliness is a sufficiently consistent and salient component of certain already diagnosable disorders that it warrants consideration as a condition secondary to or associated with an already diagnosable condition, as well as whether loneliness is a significant and salient enough condition in and of itself to merit an independent diagnosis. This is an important challenge for clinicians to become sufficiently informed about loneliness so that depression is not diagnosed and treated when loneliness may be the primary presenting problem" (8) which, as we have seen from other studies can contribute to many other severe psychological, psychiatric, behavioral, and criminal problems.

The Haggett 1999 adolescent Victim Study challenged the APA to include "Ephebophilia" as a diagnosis or differential diagnosis under the heading "Pedophilia." The Victim Study also called to the attention of the APA that "intense loneliness" as well as the entire "Differential Diagnosis" category of definitions had been eliminated completely under the description of "Pedophilia." "Loneliness" is a problem that has been previously noticed but subsequently ignored, discounted, or not deemed a pathological factor that might have more severe consequences. Our data indicate that persistent intense loneliness is keenly connected to clergy sexual abuse. It may be one aspect of sexual abuse that is connected to general public abuse as well. The difference between the two, however, is that persistent intense loneliness among the Roman Catholic clergy is largely due to enforced mandatory celibacy. While there is literature that addresses loneliness among priests, no other literature except for this paper has been found so far that specifically connects the intense loneliness of mandatory celibacy with resulting clergy sexual abuse.

Proper identification of the disorder of intense loneliness among celibate priests will promote more beneficial research in the future—crucial because with continued vague terminology and understanding of clergy sexual abuse, our data indicate that innocent children will continue to be abused, not to mention what more can result from the depraved conditions under which priests who have not received the charism or gift of celibacy/chastity will continue to be forced to live. According to Booth, "Loneliness can be an extremely debilitating way to live, and taking into account the correlates of loneliness that place patients at significant risk, serious consideration of this issue does not seem premature. It may well be that simply having people in our lives is insufficient; perhaps they need to be persons whom we perceive to be able to satisfy our needs for close, intimate contact" (2000:3).

The above Booth statement was supported recently by the following anecdotal comment from a married Protestant minister who wrote, "Parish priests have almost no friends outside the parish, and no friends in the parish. People who call you 'father' are not your 'friends.' They are to priests as clients are to psychologists or patients are to doctors. The relationship between them is a formal one defined by the roles they play as 'father' and 'laymen' in the church. Catholic clergy have it worse than most because they are not allowed to date or marry" (Letter on file).

Loos said, "Research, both qualitative and quantitative, should be forthcoming regarding this important conceptualization [depraved loneliness as Loos describes it]. Understanding the condition may lead to a reduction in recidivism" (2002:210).

Bibliography

Akerlind, Ingemar. 1992. Loneliness and alcohol abuse: A review of evidences of an interplay. *Social Science & Medicine.* 34:405–414.

Andrews, D.A., and James Bonta. 1994. *The Psychology of Criminal Conduct.* Cincinnati, OH: Anderson Publishing Co.

American Psychiatric Association: Diagnostic and Statistical Manual of Mental Disorders, DSM-IV-TR. (2000) Washington, D.C.: APA

————.1994. *American Psychiatric Association: Diagnostic and Statistical Manual of Mental Disorders, DSM-IV.* Washington, D.C.: APA

————.1987. *American Psychiatric Association: Diagnostic and Statistical Manual of Mental Disorders, DSM-IIIR.* Washington, D.C.: APA.

Arnold, Regina. 1980. "Socio-structural determinants of self-esteem and the relationship between self-esteem and criminal behavior patterns of imprisoned minority women." *U.S. Univ. Microfilms International.* 40(10A):5603.

Babbie, Earl. 1995. *The Practice of Social Research.* Belmont, CA: Wadsworth.

Baumeister, Roy F., Laura Smart, and Joseph Boden. 1999. "Relation of threatened egotism to violence and aggression: The dark side of high self-esteem." Pp. 257–272 in *Self in Social Psychology,* edited by Roy F. Baumeister. Philadelphia: Psychology Press.

Booth, Richard. 2000. Loneliness as a Component of Psychiatric Disorders. *Medscape General Medicine.* 2(2): posted 3/22/2002. Retrieved April 7, 2004.
(http://www.medscape.com/viewarticle/430545).

Brennan, Tim. 1982. "Loneliness at Adolescence." Pp. 269–290, in *Loneliness: A Sourcebook of Current Theory, Research and Therapy,* edited by Peplau, L.A. and Daniel Perlman. NY: Wiley.

CBSNews Online. 2002. Priest suicides tied to sex charges?
(http://www.CBSNEWS.com/stories/2002/05/23/national/main509970.shtmlshtml)
Retrieved July 11, 2004.

Celibacy. 2004. *America Uncover.* HBO-TV, June 28.

Coon, D. 2000. "Introduction to psychology: Exploration and application," in Ami Rokach, "Perceived causes of loneliness in adulthood." *Journal of Social Behavior & Personality.* 15:67–85.

Cozzens, Donald B. 2000. *The Changing Face of the Priesthood.* Collegeville, MN: Liturgical Press.

Dietch, James. 1978. "Love, Sex Roles and Psychological Health." *Journal of Personality Assessment.* 42:626–634.

DiTommasso, Enrico, Cyndi Brannen, and Lisa A. Best. 2004. "Measurement and Validity Characteristics of the Short Version of the Social and Emotional 'Loneliness' Scale for Adults." *Educational & Psychological Measurement.* 64:99–119.

Durkheim, E. 1951, 1897. *Suicide.* NY: Free Press.

Gill, James. 2002. In Dean Hoge, *The First Five Years of the Priesthood. A Study of Newly Ordained Catholic Priests.* Collegeville, MN: Liturgical Press.

Hackney, H. and C. G. Wrenn, Eds. 1990. "The contemporary counselor in a changed world. In: Loos, Michael, The Synergy of depravity and loneliness in alcoholism: A new conceptualization, and old problem." *Counseling & Values.* 3:199–212.

Haggett, Louise. 2000. "Is A Sexual Abusing Roman Catholic Priest a Pedophile? The Case for Ephebophilia." Presented at the 70th Annual Meeting of the Eastern Sociological Society, Baltimore Hilton, Baltimore, March 2–5.

————. 1999 "Is a Sexual Abusing Roman Catholic Priest a Pedophile? The Case for Ephebophilia." Presented at the Society for the Scientific Study of Religion and Religious Research Association's *What Do We Know about Religious Institutions and How Have We Come to Know It?"* Swissotel, Boston, November 5–7.

Haggett, Louise, Hanson, Tara, Solo, Megan. 1997. What Factors Contribute to Catholic Priests Breaking Their Vows of Celibacy/ Chastity? Unpublished.

Hill, C.T., Z. Rubin, and L.A. Peplau, L. A. 1976. "Breakups before marriage: The end of 102 affairs." In Jones, Warren: "Loneliness and Social Behavior" in *Loneliness. A Sourcebook of Current Theory, Research and Therapy,* edited by Lititia Anne Peplau and Daniel Perlman, . NY: Wiley.

Hoge, Dean R. 2002. *The First Five Years of the Priesthood. A Study of Newly Ordained Catholic Priests.* Collegeville, MN: The Liturgical Press.

Jones, Warren H. 1982. "Loneliness and Social Behavior." Ch. 15 in *Loneliness. A Sourcebook of Current Theory, Research and Therapy,* edited by Lititia Anne Peplau and Daniel Perlman. NY: Wiley.

Jones, W. H. and M.D. Carver. 1991. "Adjustment and coping implications of loneliness," in: Jari-Erik Nurmi, Sari Toivonen, Katariina Salmela-Aro, and Sana Eronen. 1997. "Social Strategies and Loneliness." *Journal of Social Psychology.* 137:764–778.

Jones, Warren H., R.O. Hansson, and T.G.

Smith. 1980. "Loneliness and love: Implications for psychological and interpersonal functioning, in Loneliness and Social Behavior."

Loneliness. A Sourcebook of Current Theory, Research and Therapy, edited by Lititia Anne Peplau and Daniel Perlman. NY: Wiley

Kim, Oksoo. 1997. "Loneliness: A predictor of health perceptions among older Korean immigrants." *Psychological Reports.* 81:591–594.

Kornblum, Janet. 2005. For Steinem, these are the glory years. *USA Today,* February 2.

Loos, Michael D. 2002. "The synergy of depravity and loneliness in alcoholism: A new conceptualization, and old problem." *Counseling & Values.* 46:199–212.

Marsa, Fiona, Gary O'Reilly, Alan Carr, Paul Murphy, Maura O'Sullivan, Anthony Cotter, and Davi Hevey. 2004. "Attachment Styles and Psychological Profiles of Child Sex Offenders in Ireland." *Journal of Interpersonal Violence.* 19:228–251.

Marshall, W.L. 1989. "Intimacy, loneliness and sexual offenders," in Rokach, Ami. 2001. "Criminal offense type and the causes of 'loneliness'." *Journal of Psychology.* 135:277–291.

Maslow, Abraham H. 1987, 1954. *Motivation and Personality.* NY: Harper & Row.

Medora, Nilufer P.; John C. Woodward. 1991. "Factors associates with loneliness among alcoholics in rehabilitation centers." *Journal of Social Psychology.* 131: 769–779).

National Opinion Research Center (NORC). 1972. *The Catholic priest in the United States: Sociological investigations.* Andrew Greeley and Richard A. Schoenherr, principal investigators. Washington, D.C.: US Catholic Conference.

Nurmi, Jari-Erik, Sari Toivonen, Katariina Salmela-Aro, and Sana Eronen. 1997. "Social Strategies and Loneliness." *Journal of Social Psychology.* 137:764–778.

Peplau, Lititia Anne, Daniel Perlman, eds. 1982. *Loneliness. A Sourcebook of Current Theory, Research and Therapy.* NY: Wiley

Rice, David.1990. *Shattered Vows. Priests Who Leave.* NY: Triumph Books.

Rokach, Ami. 2001. "Criminal offense type and the causes of loneliness." *Journal of Psychology.* 135:277–291.

———. 2000a. "Offense type and the experience of 'loneliness'." *International Journal of Offender Therapy & Comparative Criminology.* 44:549–563.

———. 2000b. "Perceived Causes of Loneliness in Adulthood." *Journal of Social Behavior & Personality.* 15:67–85.

———. 1990. "Surviving and coping with 'loneliness'." *Journal of Psychology.* 124:39–54.

Rokach, Ami, Heather, Brock. 1997. Loneliness: A multidimensional experience. *Psychology: A Journal of Human Behavior.* 34(1):1–9.

Rokach, Ami, Koledin, Spomenka. (1997). "Loneliness in jail: A study of the loneliness of incarcerated men." *International Journal of Offender Therapy & Comparative Criminology.* 4:168–179.

Rook, K.S. "Research on social support loneliness and social isolation: Toward an integration," in: Akerlind, Ingemar. 1992. "'Loneliness' and alcohol abuse: A review of evidences of an interplay." *Social Science & Medicine.* 34:405–414.

Rossetti, Stephen J. 1994. "Priest Suicides and the Crisis of Faith." *America Magazine,* October 29.

Rubinstein, C. and Shaver, P. 1980. "Loneliness in two northeastern cities," in *The Anatomy of Loneliness,* edited by J. Hortag and J. Andy. NY: International Universities Press.

Russell, Daniel. 1982. "The Measurement of loneliness." Ch. 6, in *Loneliness. A Sourcebook of Current Theory, Research and Therapy,* edited by Peplau, Lititia Anne, Daniel Perlman. NY: Wiley

Russell, Daniel, L. A. Peplau, and C. Cutrona. 1980. "The revised UCLA Loneliness Scale: Concurrent and discriminant validity evidence," in Jones, Warren H. (1982). Loneliness and Social Behavior. Ch. 15 in *Loneliness. A Sourcebook of Current Theory, Research and Therapy,* edited by. Lititia Anne Peplau and Daniel Perlman. NY: Wiley.

Schneider, Hans. 1997. "Sexual abuse of children: Strengths and weaknesses of current criminology." *International Journal of Offender Therapy & Comparative Criminology.* 41:310–324.

Schoenherr, Richard A. and David Yamane. 2002. *Goodbye Father.* NY: Oxford.

Schoenherr, Richard A and Lawrence A. Young. 1993. *Full Pews and Empty Altars.* WI: University of Wisconsin Press.

Sipe, A. W. Richard. 2003. *Celibacy in Crisis. A Secret World Revisited.* NY: Brunner Routledge.

————.1995. *Sex, Priests and Power. Anatomy of a Crisis.* NY: Brunner Mazel.

————.1990. *A Secret World: Sexuality and the Search for Celibacy.* NY: Brunner Mazel.

Turner, Jonathan H. 1995. *Sociological Theory.* Belmont, CA: Wadsworth Publishing.

Weiss, R.S. 1982. "Issues in the study of loneliness." Ch. 5 in *Loneliness. A Sourcebook of Current Theory, Research and Therapy*, edited by Lititia Anne Peplau and Daniel Perlman. NY: Wiley

————. 1973. "Loneliness: The experience of emotional and social isolation." In: Jones, Warren H. 1982. "Loneliness and Social Behavior." Ch. 15 in *Loneliness. A Sourcebook of Current Theory, Research and Therapy*, edited by Lititia Anne Peplau and Daniel Perlman. NY: Wiley.

West, Donald A., Robert Kellner and Maggi Moore-West. 1986. "The effects of 'loneliness': A review of the literature." *Comprehensive Psychiatry.* 27:351–363.

Wilkes, Paul. 1991. "Profiles. The Education of an Archbishop II (Rembert Weakland)." *The New Yorker,* July 22.

7

General Conclusion

It has been difficult for the research community to identify a causal relationship regarding clergy sexual abuse in part because of the inconsistent research that has taken place regarding child sexual abuse in general, but also because of the vague language used by the church in public documents on celibacy and chastity in the priesthood.

The public is led to believe that celibacy in the priesthood means abstinence from sex. Reality is quite a different thing: it literally means being unmarried, else bishops would not be so lenient. An example occurred in the July 2004 MSNBC program on celibacy in which the interviewer asked a priest who announced his leaving because of mandatory celibacy, whether or not he had "strayed from his vow of celibacy," meaning "had he had sex?" He replied that he is "not married" and has "remained single" (*Celibacy and the Church 2004*). Chastity—sexual abstinence—was never mentioned by the priest. This attitude prevailed in the Priest Study as well: some priests went to the trouble of explaining the difference when asked about celibacy and chastity. (See comments from priests at the end of chapter 2.)

The relatively new public knowledge that priests have been promiscuous would indicate that the vow of chastity is not being adhered to by those who take it and that sexual partners have apparently been easy to get, either through clandestine or abusive relationships. Meaningful relationships, on the other hand, are what they lack as celibate priests, denying them the opportunity to date and marry.

The church has ignored and covered up sexual indiscretions and wrongdoing, indeed criminal behavior, by some of its celibate clergy, yet has cut off from ministry and retirement pensions anyone who has had the integrity to marry or partner—two hundred thousand worldwide in over thirty years (Antony 2004). These men who entered the priesthood because of a truly divine calling and later suffered intense loneliness or because of mandatory celibacy left their clerical ministry—many during the first five years (Hoge 2002, Schoenherr and Young 1990, 1993); others who also struggled apparently went the route of clandestine or abusive relationships. For the latter, the hierarchy's "blind eye" was a green light until they got caught.

Evidence in *The Bingo Report* indicates that both the profiles of the majority of priest perpetrators and the characteristics of sexual abuse that they inflicted are too different to suggest any similarities between clergy sexual abuse and sexual abuse in other segments of society. The only exception would be the sexual abuse of female adults (approximately one-third of female clergy abuse victims), characteristics of which mirror the general population studies.

We conclude that just as loneliness/depression/low self-esteem/ substance abuse/ crime/suicide are overlapping problems in general society, the problem of clergy sexual abuse is related to loneliness, however more intense because of mandatory celibacy. The following "organizational chart" illustrates the effects of enforced celibacy in the Catholic Church described in this paper.

Our data indicate that for the majority of priest sexual perpetrators, the abuse is more a result of the length of time they are forced to live without an intimate relationship, be it male or female, than it is a preexisting condition. We therefore conclude that, with the

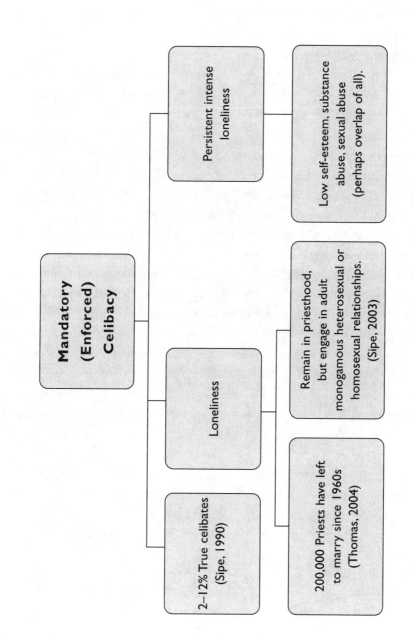

exception of a few extreme cases, the majority of perpetrators are not pedophiles or ephebophiles when they first enter into the priesthood.

Whether or not priest perpetrators are "abused abusers" (were victims themselves) is a question for future study. A suggestion was made by a priest respondent/survivor in the Victim Study that CSRI poll the priest population to see how many had been abused in seminary. A national support organization is forming in 2005 for priests who are victims of priests.

This report does not cover the psychological aspects of priests, such as their psychosexuality, a subject that has been discussed by acclaimed celibacy researchers and authors, such as psychologist A. W. Richard Sipe (2003, 1995, 1990) and Eugene Kennedy et al (1977). Their studies are related to the immaturity of priests that arises because of underdeveloped psychosexuality after becoming seminarians at 12 or 13 years of age. This recruitment practice however, is less likely to happen today, versus thirty or forty years ago. Sipe links sexual immaturity in priests psychologically to the age of adolescent victims.

Questions that may invite future research: Why do some priests stay and others leave the active ministry when they struggle with mandatory celibacy? Is it because of their pension, or fear of being unable to find another job, or even having to "go to work"? Do they prefer to live a free but double life? Do bishops put fear in priests' minds about transitioning to secular society? Do priests rationalize the breaking of vows? Do they think they can just go to confession and receive forgiveness? Do bishops and priests think that as spiritual leaders, they are above the law? Are the weak ones among those who struggle with mandatory celibacy the ones who stay?

Why have the bishops committed a pattern of alleged crimes in aiding and abetting the abuse that has taken place? Could one reason be that they too have suffered from intense loneliness and, therefore, understand the problems that priests are facing?

Larger independent, interdisciplinary studies are recommended for the Roman Catholic clergy who are still in the church system including priests in treatment centers, as well as convicted priests incarcerated for sexual abuse. Specific independent testing is urged from many perspectives regarding intense loneliness: medical, social science, behavioral, anthropological, and criminal—tests such as Personal Orientation Inventory (Shostrom 1966), Loneliness Scale (Russell, Peplau and Cutrona 1980; Richardson 2004), Life Satisfaction Index-Z (Wood, Wylie and Shaefor 1969, or more current versions). Relative to the loneliness analysis, more specific responses regarding frequency of loneliness will be crucial in measuring the intensity of loneliness that a celibate priest may suffer, determining whether or not pathology exists. It would be recommended that as precise a response option as possible be included.

Clergy sexual abuse is not a new problem in the Catholic Church. According to authors of a new book, *Priests, Sex and Secret Files*, Thomas Doyle and A. W. Richard Sipe (2005) clergy sexual abuse "clearly demonstrates a deep-seated problem that spans the Church's (entire) history. The collection of documents and official and unofficial sources begins its survey in the first century and concludes with the contemporary scandal" (News release, March 2005).

In 1139, the following statement was made by Bishop Imola of Italy during the celibacy debates: "When celibacy is imposed, priests will commit sins far worse than fornication. Since some men cannot live by the council [sic] of perfect chastity, they will seek sexual release wherever they can find it" (Barstow 1982:112).

Recent research regarding celibate Japanese monks has provided evidence that one hundred years ago at the turn of the twentieth century, the Japanese government abolished mandatory celibacy among Japanese monks because of the deviant behavior that was taking place among them (Jaffe 2001).

The church is in financial jeopardy, and parishes are being sold in order to pay settlements. Beyond the psychological and spiritual damage done to the victims and their families, the effects are threatening the viability of the institution.

This report in no way condones the behavior of priests convicted of large-scale sexual abuse. In fact, we are not excusing *any* sexual crime already committed by any priest against children and/ or adults. As moral leaders, they teach the difference between good and evil and how to choose good over evil. They, therefore, should know the difference themselves and have made the choice themselves, knowing there may be criminal consequences.

Bibliography

Akerlind, Ingemar. 1992. "'Loneliness' and alcohol abuse: A review of evidences of interplay." *Social Science & Medicine.* 34:405–414.

Arroyo, Raymond, narrator. 2004. National Review Board Report on Clergy Sexual Abuse. EWTN Television Network, February 27.

Barstow, Anne Llewellyn. 1982. *Married Priests and the Reforming Papacy—The Eleventh-Century Debates.* NY. Edwin Mellon Press

Bateson, Gregory. 1972. *Steps to an Ecology of Mind.* NY: Ballantine.

Celibacy & the Church. 2004. MSNBC-TV, July 7.

Coriden, James A., Green, Thomas J., and Heintschel, Donald E. 1985. *The Code of Canon Law: A text and commentary.* Mahwah, NJ: Paulist Press.

Doyle, Thomas P and A.W. Richard Sipe. 2005. *Priests, Sex, and Secret Files.* (to be released August, 2005).

Goldman, Alan H. 1977. "Plain Sex." *Philosophy & Public Affairs.* 6:267–287.

Haggett, Louise. 2000. "Is A Sexual Abusing Roman Catholic Priest a Pedophile? The Case for Ephebophilia." Presented at the 70th Annul Meeting of the Eastern Sociological Society, Baltimore Hilton, Baltimore, March 2–5.

———. 1999 "Is a Sexual Abusing Roman Catholic Priest a Pedophile? The Case for Ephebophilia." Presented at the Society for the Scientific Study of Religion and Religious Research Association's What Do We Know about Religious Institutions and How Have We Come to Know It?" Swissotel, Boston, November 5–7.

Haggett, Louise, Hanson, Tara, Solo, Megan. 1997. "What Factors Contribute to Catholic Priests Breaking Their Vows of Celibacy/Chastity?" Unpublished.

Hoge, Dean R. 2002. The First Five Years of the Priesthood. A Study of Newly Ordained Catholic Priests. Collegeville, MN: The Liturgical Press.

Jaffe, Richard M. 2001. *Neither Monk nor Layman: Clerical marriage in modern Japanese Buddhism.* NJ: Princeton University Press.

Kennedy, Eugene C., V.J. Heckler, F.J. Kobler and R.E. Walker. 1977. "Clinical assessment of a profession: Roman Catholic clergymen." *Journal of Clinical Psychology.* 33:120–128.

Lynch, Gerald W., Michele Galietta, Margaret Leland Smith, James Levine, Maureen O'Connor, Steven Penrod, Louis Schlesinger and Karen Terry. 2004. *The Nature and Scope of Sexual Abuse of Minors by Catholic Priests and Deacons in the United States 1950–2002.* The John Jay College of Criminal Justice. NY.

Richardson, John D. 2004. "Isolating frequency scale effects on self-reported loneliness." *Personality & Individual Differences.* 36:235–244.

Russell, Daniel, Peplau, L.A., Cutrona, C. 1980. "The revised UCLA Loneliness Scale: Concurrent and discriminant validity evidence." Vol.39. *Journal of Personality and Social Psychology, in Loneliness and Social Behavior (Jones, ibid)*

Schoenherr, Richard A & Young, Lawrence A. 1993. *Full Pews and Empty Altars.* WI: University of Wisconsin Press.

———. 1990. "Quitting the Clergy: Resignations in the Roman Catholic Priesthood." *Journal for the Scientific Study of Religion.* 29:463–481.

Sipe, A. W. Richard. 2003. *Celibacy In Crisis. A Secret World Revisited.* NY: Brunner Routledge.

———. 1995. *Sex, Priests and Power. Anatomy of a Crisis.* NY: Brunner Mazel.

———. 1990. *A Secret World: Sexuality and the Search for Celibacy.* NY: Brunner Mazel.

Staff Reports. 2004. Bishops accused of sexual misconduct. CST, January 21.

(http://www.wfaa.com/s/dws/spe/2002/bishops/stories/061202dnmetbishside.1d915.html)

Retrieved March 14, 2004.

Wood, V. Wylie, M.F. and Shaefor, B. 1969. An analysis of short self-report measures of life satisfaction: correlation with rater judgments. *Journal of Gerontology.* 2:465–469.

8

How Much Does the Church Know?

We recently came into possession of a transcribed speech given in 1990 to the U.S. Conference of Bishops by civil and canon lawyer Bishop A. James Quinn. Excerpts have already appeared in books and general news articles regarding clergy sexual abuse. (Berry 1990; McCarty 2002; Hogan-Albach 2004). These and other news accounts told of the Bishop's instructions to other members of the hierarchy regarding the hiding of clergy abuse evidence in the church's secret archives. What may have been less noticed from this same speech, however, are Bishop Quinn's comments regarding intense loneliness suffered by many priests, which he indicated was due to mandatory celibacy. According to Bishop Quinn:

> *Biological causes: Biology plays a role. Clinicians and researchers accept the fact that the force behind the sex drive is clearly biological. Dr. Fred Berlin of Johns Hopkins uses a language example to illustrate the point that people do not choose the nature of their sexual desires anymore than they determine the language in which they are going to think and speak. Dr. Berlin compares the difficulty in resisting biological sex urges with the difficulty*

that the overeaters have in resisting food. And Dr. Money, a researcher also at Johns Hopkins, developed a theory espousing sexual orientation developing "in utero,[sic]" and that theory was supported by Dr. Michael Peterson. Some of you may know him. But most clinicians believe in some biological influence, but they don't think that there is evidence as yet to support the utero theory. Abnormalities in some pedophiles, however, do include chromosomal anomalies, abnormal testosterone levels, hormonal irregularities, abnormal CT scans (Cat Scans), pathological EG's and others. Positron Emission Telegraphy, called PET, is a new technology that is being used in the study of pedophilia, and it measures the chemical change in the brain when sexual arousal takes place, and for some people sex seems to have almost addictive qualities, and if changes in the brain can be identified clearly then comparisons could possibly be made between individuals with and without various sexual disorders. Thus, it seems plausible to accept the theory that biology plays some essential role in the development of sexual orientation and affectional preferences.

Psychological causes and considerations: This is an area of current research. It's common for a priest to talk about his loneliness and reveal that his sexual acting out was an attempt to meet his human need for contact and attachment, his craving for emotional closeness to someone in his life. The pedophile is often confused about sexuality versus intimacy. He often needs help in clarifying the difference. He needs help in understanding that being genitally active does not provide the intimacy that he seeks. Efforts are being made through the testing of these patients to gather evidence that might show that psychological or psycho-sexual development of the pedophile has the sexual psychology of a seven year old; then we can't deal with that person as if he were a normally mature adult. Dealing with pedophilia: Denial and guilt frequently play an important role in a pedophile's life. The pedophile often minimizes the erotic component of his behavior. The initial goal of treatment is to help a pedophile understand the sexuality inherent in the behavior that he is involved in. And here again we are dealing with basic human needs. A desire for intimacy, for closeness, for companionship, and denial can easily lead a person to an almost fantasy life existence where he does not see the overall consequences of his behavior.

The above paragraphs were reported verbatim from Bishop Quinn's speech rather than excerpted, in order to avoid any confusion regarding the bishop's statement.

The conclusions reached in *The Bingo Report* had apparently been known by the hierarchy of the church since at least 1990, hidden away from the public and the court system, as well as hidden from its own priests and seminarians. The Quinn speech validates our research and *The Bingo Report*, providing further evidence of the Catholic hierarchy's culpability in aiding and abetting sexual abuse and that they may be responsible for not only the psychological damage of the clergy abuse victims, but also psychological damage to its own clergy.

The final question that needs to be asked is, "What is the extent, the prevalence of clergy sexual abuse?"

The John Jay College Report (JJCR) (Lynch, 2004) indicated that, based on their surveys, 3% to 6% of priests were perpetrators of sexual abuse of minors (16). JJCR also provided percentages of victims per priests, based their findings of formal and "potential" (file evidence with no formal complaint) allegations.

JJCR reported two total priest populations from 1950 to 2002: 109,694, the number provided by the Catholic hierarchy and 94,607 from the Center of Applied Research in the Apostolate (CARA, Georgetown University) (18). The discrepancy with the higher church figure may be because priests are sometimes accounted for by more than one diocese in any given year depending on which diocese they came from and which seminary they attended, where they were ordained or where they were transferred (Kenedy Directory). Although the CARA estimate may be more accurate, we will use an average of the two—102,151.

The following calculations represent 3% to 6% of the average total number of priests from 1950 to 2002, multiplied by the categories of number of victims per priest, as supplied by JJCR based on their survey results:

Average number of priests 1950-2002 = 102,151

Percentage of perpetrators 1950-2002 = 3% to 6%

Number of victims per priest 1950-2002 = 50%/1 victim, 26.4%/ 2-3 victims (average 2.5), 17.8%/4-9 victims (average 6.5), 5.8%/10+ victims with an average of 14, according to JJCR (41).

3% of total priests (102,151) as perpetrators = 3,065 priest perpetrators 1950-2002

3,065 priest perpetrators x 50% = 1,533 x 1 victim each	=	1,533
3,065 priest perpetrators x 26.4% = 809 x 2.5% victims each	=	2,023
3,065 priest perpetrators x 17.8% = 546 x 6.5% victims each	=	3,549
3,065 priest perpetrators x 5.8% = 178 x 14 victims each	=	2,492
Total adolescent victims		**9,597**

6% of total priests 102,151) as perpetrators = 6,129 priest perpetrators 1950-2002

6,129 priest perpetrators x 50% = 3,065 x 1 victim each	=	3,065
6,129 priest perpetrators x 26.4% = 1,618 x 2.5% victims each	=	4,045
6,129 priest perpetrators x 17.8% = 1,091 x 6.5% victims each	=	7,092
6,129 priest perpetrators x 5.8% = 355 x 14 victims each	=	4,970
Total adolescent victims		**19,172**

Our own victim study revealed almost 1/3 more adult victims. If we add 33% to each of the above numbers, new totals would be: at 3%, 12,764 victims; and at 6%, 25,500 victims.

After analyzing 19 child sexual abuse studies among the general population, Finkelhor (1994) wrote, "Less than one-third of all occurring cases are currently identified and substantiated (34)." He estimated that prevalence is three times the incidence factor (chapter 3). If we apply the same three-times formula to establish prevalence in the priesthood, 12,764 would become 38,292 and the 25,500 figure would climb to 76,500 in the U.S. Considering that the JJCR included surveys ending in 2002, hundreds or perhaps thousands more reports have surfaced since then, making these estimates conservative. One example involves the fall 2005 revelations in the Philadelphia diocese where a grand jury report indicates that complaints had been leveled against 169 priests. The chancery said the figure is 54 (McCoy 2005).

According to the *World Almanac* (2005), U.S. Catholics comprise only 6.6% (66 million) of the world's Catholic population of 1 billion. Based on the Finkelhor three-times formula, this means that the world-wide prevalence of all Catholic clergy victims is somewhere between: at 3%, 580,181 victims; and at 6%, 1,159,000 victims.

Costs to Catholics

As of 2005, the total direct costs look to exceed $2 to $3 billion because of the many additional victims coming forward with their stories of clergy abuse (Kusmer, 2005). In terms of priests' treatment, JJC indicated that the average is 1.2 times per priest (Lynch, 87). Stephen Rossetti of St. Luke's Institute, one of the main treatment facilities, said such treatment costs approximately $350 per day per priest and that average treatment lasts between 4 and 7 months (*The Plain Dealer,* 2002). At 1.2 times per priest, the following shows what this has cost the Catholic Church up to 2002 in the U.S. alone:

At 3%

4 months (122 days) x 3065 priests x $350 per day = $130,875,500

7 months (273 days) x 3065 priests x $350 per day = $292,860,750

At 6%

4 months (122 days) x 6129 priests x $350 per day = $261,708,300

7 months (273 days) x 6129 priests x $350 per day = $585,625,950

According to JJCR, ***only 22% of these amounts are covered by medical insurance*** (94). Catholic contributions have been paying the difference.

Between 1950 and 2002, total attorney costs for legal representation was $38.5 million (not including Boston), representing only 60%

of the dioceses surveyed since 40% did not respond to the question (Lynch, 93). If we add the other 40%, total legal fees would be approximately $64 million. *None of the $64 million is covered by insurance*. In addition, *only 22% of U.S. victim treatment was covered by insurance and 43% of U.S. victim compensation was covered by insurance (Lynch, 93).*

The following large settlements are an example of settlements that are not part of the above figures because they are more recent than the JJCR time frame:

Boston	$85 million
Orange, CA	$100 million
Covington, KY	$120 million
Portland, OR	$500 million
Los Angeles	$500 million to $1.5 billion

From a psychological perspective, Catholic clergy abuse will go down in history as one of the world's horror stories. From a financial perspective, it may fall into the category of financial disasters or misappropriations of funds like Enron, Tyco and others. The major difference, however, is that this is an IRS designated charity and the dollars used to pay for the after-effect of clergy sexual abuse are tax-deductible contributions made with the intent of assisting in the good works of the Catholic Church. Even more disturbing is the fact that the majority of non serial clergy sexual abuse crimes against our innocent could have been prevented.

Bibliography

Berry, Jason. 1992. *Lead Us Not Into Temptation. Catholic priests and the sexual abuse of children.* NY: Doubleday.

Economus, Thomas. 1995. *Missing Link,* Fall.

Egerton, Books, Reese Dunklin. 2002. Bishops accused of sexual misconduct. *The Dallas Morning News,* June 12.

Finkelhor, David. 1994. Current information on the scope and nature of child sexual abuse. *The Future of Children. Sexual Abuse of Children.* 2:31-53.

Hogan-Albach, Susan. 2004. USCCB committee bishops accused of abuse cover-up. 3 members of panel named in lawsuits; criticism called unfair. *Dallas Morning News,* January 19.

Kusmer, Ken. 2005. Group says abuse scandal could cost $2 billion or more. Associated Press. July 9.
http://abcnews.go.com/US/wireStory?id=924538

Lynch, Gerald W., Michele Galietta, Margaret Leland Smith, James Levine, Maureen O'Connor, Steven Penrod, Louis Schlesinger, Karen Terry. 2004. *The Nature and Scope of Sexual Abuse of Minors by Catholic Priests and Deacons in the United States 1050-2002.* The John Jay College of Criminal Justice.

McCarthy, James F. 2002. Bishop Quinn exits abuse panel. *Cleveland Plain Dealer,* September 10.

McCoy, Craig R. 2005. Complaints involved 169 priests. *Philadelphia Inquirer,* Sept. 25.
(http://go.philly.com/mid/inquirer/news/local/states/pennsylvania/12732404.htm)
Retrieved September 30, 2005.

Plain Dealer, The. 2002. The Cost of Abuse. Dioceses across U.S. sell land, borrow millions. March 11.
(http://www.cleveland.com/abuse/index.ssf?/abuse/more/101584981241649.html)
Retrieved July 18, 2005.

Quinn, A. James. 1991. NCCB Guidelines and other considerations in pedophilia cases. Presented in 1990 in Columbus, Ohio, at the Midwest Canon Law Society.

World Almanac. 2005. NY: World Almanac Books.

World Book Encyclopedia. 2005. Chicago: World Books, Inc.

References in alphabetical order:

Abel, Gene G. and Joanne L. Rouleau. 1995. "Sexual abuses. Special Issue: Clinical sexuality." *Psychiatric Clinics of North America,* 1:139–153.

AFP. 1995. "Tough Pedophilia Bill Derailed." *International Herald Tribune,* November 8.

Akerlind, Ingemar. 1992. Loneliness and alcohol abuse: A review of evidences of an interplay. *Social Science & Medicine.* 34:405–414.

Akers, Ronald L. 1985. *Deviant Behavior: A Social Learning Perspective.* Belmont, CA: Wadsworth.

American Humane Association. 1996. *Fact Sheet.* Children's Division, AHA.

American Psychiatric Association: Diagnostic and Statistical Manual of Mental Disorders, DSM-IV-TR. 2000. Washington, D.C. APA.

———. 1994. *American Psychiatric Association: Diagnostic and Statistical Manual of Mental Disorders, DSM-IV.* Washington, D.C.: APA

———. 1987. *American Psychiatric Association: Diagnostic and Statistical Manual of Mental Disorders, DSM-IIIR.* Washington, D.C.: APA.

Ames, M. Ashley and David A. Houston. 1990. Legal, "Social, and Biological Definitions of Pedophilia." *Archives of Sexual Behavior,* 4:333–342.

Anderson, Kenneth N., Lois E. Anderson, and Walter D. Glanze. 1994. *Mosby's Medical, Nursing & Allied Health Dictionary.* St. Louis, MO: Mosby.

Andrews, D.A., and James Bonta. 1994. *The Psychology of Criminal Conduct.* Cincinnati, OH: Anderson Publishing Co.

Arnold, Regina. 1980. "Socio-structural determinants of self-esteem and the relationship between self-esteem and criminal behavior patterns of imprisoned minority women." *U.S. Univ. Microfilms International.* 40(10A):5603.

Arroyo, Raymond, narrator. 2004. "National Review Board Report on Clergy Sexual Abuse." EWTN Television Network, February 27.

Associated Press. 1998. Pentagon Estimates Viagra Costs $50M. *The Union Leader.* Manchester, NH, October 3.

Babbie, Earl. 1995. *The Practice of Social Research.* Belmont, CA: Wadsworth.

Barstow, Anne Llewellyn. 1982. *Married Priests and the Reforming Papacy—The Eleventh-Century Debates.* NY. Edwin Mellon Press

Baumeister, Roy F., Laura Smart, and Joseph Boden. 1999. "Relation of threatened egotism to violence and aggression: The dark side of high self-esteem." Pp. 257–272 in *Self in Social Psychology,* edited by Roy F. Baumeister. Philadelphia: Psychology Press.

Bates, Frederick and Katherine S. van Wormer. 1979. "A Study of Leadership Roles in an Alabama Prison for Women." *Human Relations.* 9:793–801.

Bateson, Gregory. 1972. *Steps to an Ecology of Mind.* NY: Ballantine.

Bennetts, Leslie. 1991. Unholy Acts. *Vanity Fair,* December.

Berry, Jason. 1992. *Lead Us Not Into Temptation. Catholic priests and the sexual abuse of children.* NY: Doubleday.

Blumer, Herbert. 1969. *Symbolic Interactionism: Perceptions and Method.* NJ: Prentice-Hall.

Bonnike, Frank J., James Gower and Louise Haggett. 1993. "The Movement, the Ministries & the Methods." Workshop presented at the 25th Annual National Federation of Priests Council (NFPC) Convention & House of Delegates. Chicago, IL, May 3–7.

Booth, Richard. 2000. Loneliness as a Component of Psychiatric Disorders. *Medscape General Medicine.* 2(2): posted 3/22/2002. Retrieved April 7, 2004. *(http://www.medscape.com/viewarticle/430545).*

Brennan, Tim. 1982. "Loneliness at Adolescence." Pp. 269–290, in *Loneliness: A Sourcebook of Current Theory, Research and Therapy,* edited by Peplau, L.A. and Daniel Perlman. NY: Wiley.

Briere, John and Marsha Runtz. 1989. "University Males' Sexual Interest in Children: Predicting Potential Indices of 'Pedophilia' in a Nonforensic Sample." *Child Abuse & Neglect.*13:65–75.

Burkett, Elixir and Frank Bruni. 1993. *Gospel of Shame.* NY: Penguin.

Cameron, P., W. Coburn, Jr., and H. Larson. 1986. "Child molestation and homosexuality." *Psychological Reports.* 58:327–37.

CBSNews Online. 2002. Priest suicides tied to sex charges? *(http://www.CBSNEWS.com/stories/2002/05/23/ national/main509970.shtmlshtml)* Retrieved July 11, 2004.

Celibacy. 2004. *America Uncover.* HBO-TV, June 28.

Celibacy & the Church. 2004. MSNBC-TV, July 7.

Connors, Fr. Canice. 1993. "The Issue of Sexual Misconduct & the Clergy." Workshop presented at the 25th Annual National Federation of Priests Council (NFPC) Convention & House of Delegates. Chicago, IL, May 3–7.

Coon, D. 2000. "Introduction to psychology: Exploration and application," in Ami Rokach, "Perceived causes of loneliness in adulthood." *Journal of Social Behavior & Personality.* 15:67–85.

Coridin, James A., Thomas G. Green, and Donald E. Heintschel. 1985. *The Code of Canon Law. A text and commentary.* Mahwah, NJ: Paulist Press.

Cozzens, Donald B. 2000. *The Changing Face of the Priesthood.* Collegeville, MN: Liturgical Press.

Crosby, Michael H. 1996. *Celibacy—Means of Control or Mandate of the Heart?* Notre Dame, IN: Ave Maria Press.

CST. 2004. "Bishops accused of sexual misconduct." *(http://www.WFAA.com/s/dws/spe/2002/bishops/ stories/061202dnmetbishide.1d 915.html).*

Dabrow, Allan M. 1970. "Comment—The Pros and Cons of Conjugal Visits in Prison Institutions." *Journal of Family Law.* 9: 436–440.

Diamant, Louis. 1993. *Homosexual issues in the workplace.* Philadelphia, PA: Taylor & Francis.

Dietch, James. 1978. "Love, Sex Roles and Psychological Health." *Journal of Personality Assessment.* 42:626–634.

DiTommasso, Enrico, Cyndi Brannen, and Lisa A. Best. 2004. "Measurement and Validity Characteristics of the Short Version of the Social and Emotional 'Loneliness' Scale for Adults.' *Educational & Psychological Measurement.* 64:99–119.

Doyle, Thomas P and A.W. Richard Sipe. 2005. *Priests, Sex, and Secret Files.* (to be released August, 2005).

Durkheim, E. 1951, 1897. *Suicide.* NY: Free Press.

Economus, Thomas. 1995. *Missing Link,* Fall.

Egerton, Books, Reese Dunklin. 2002. Bishops accused of sexual misconduct. *The Dallas Morning News,* June 12.

Finkelhor, David. 1994. "Current Information on the Scope and Nature of Child Sexual Abuse." *The Future of Children. Sexual Abuse of Children.* 2:31–53.

———. 1989. "Early and Long-term Effects of Child Sexual Abuse: An Update." *Professional Psychology: Research and Practice.* 21: 325–330.

Finkelhor, David and Sharon Araji. 1986. "Explanations of Pedophilia: A four factor model." *Journal of Sexual Research.* 22:145–161.

Finkelhor, David and L. Baron. 1986. "High-risk Children." Pp. 60–88 in *A Sourcebook on Child Sexual Abuse.* Edited by D. Finkelhor. Beverly Hills, CA: Sage.

Finkelhor, David, G. Hotaling, I. A. Lewis and C. Smith. 1990. "Sexual Abuse in a National Survey of Adult Men and Women: Prevalence, Characteristics, and Risk Factors." *Child Abuse & Neglect.* 14:19–28.

Finkelhor, David and Lisa Jones. 2004. "Explanations for the decline in child sexual abuse cases." *Office of Juvenile Justice and Delinquency Prevention/ OJJDP Juvenile Justice Bulletin,* January 2004. [Online] Retrieved February 27, 2004.

Fischer, David R. 1975, in Peterson, Richard A. (1979). "Revitalizing the Culture Concept." *1979 Annual Review of Sociology.*

Fraze, Barb. 1993. "Canadian Bishops move vigorously on sex abuse problems." *National Catholic Reporter,* July 3.

French, Laurence. 1979. "Prison Sexualization: Inmate Adaptations to Psychosexual Stress." *Corrective & Social Psychiatry & Journal of Behavior Technology, Methods & Therapy.* 25:64–69.

Freund, Kurt and Robin Watson. 1992. "The Proportions of Heterosexual and Homosexual Pedophiles among Sex Offenders against Children: An Exploratory Study." *Journal of Sex & Marital Therapy.* 1:34–43.

Geyelin, Milo. 1993. "The Catholic Church Struggles with Suits over Sexual Abuse." *Wall Street Journal,* November 24.

Gifis, Steven H. 1996. *Law Dictionary.* Happauge, NY: Barron's.

Gill, James. 2002. In Dean Hoge, *The First Five Years of the Priesthood. A Study of Newly Ordained Catholic Priests.* Collegeville, MN: Liturgical Press.

Gill, Fr. James. 1993. "Human Sexuality, the Priesthood, and a Mature Laity." *The American Catholic Northeast,* October.

Goldman, Alan H. 1977. "Plain Sex." *Philosophy & Public Affairs.* 6:267–287.

Gosselin, Henry. 1996. Who's Sitting in the Pews? *Church World.* 35:4

Greenberg, David M., John Bradford, and Susan Curry. 1995. "Infantophilia —A New Subcategory of Pedophilia? A Preliminary Study." *Bull American Academy Psychiatry Law.* 1:63–70.

Groth, Nicholas A., William F. Hobson, and Thomas S. Gary. 1982. *The Child Molester: Clinical Observations.* NY: Barron's.

Grubin, Don. 1992. "Sexual Offending: a cross-cultural comparison." *Annual Review of Sex Research.* (3)201–217.

Hackney, H. and C. G. Wrenn, Eds. 1990. "The contemporary counselor in a changed world. In: Loos, Michael, The Synergy of depravity and loneliness in alcoholism: A new conceptualization, and old problem." *Counseling & Values.* 3:199–212.

Haggett, Louise. 2000. "Is a sexually abusing Roman Catholic priest a pedophile? The case for ephebophilia." Presented at the 70th Annual Meeting of the Eastern Sociological Society, Baltimore Hilton, Baltimore, March 2–5.

———. 1999. ibid. Presented at the Society for the Scientific Study of Religion and Religious Research Association's *"What Do We Know about Religious Institutions and How Have We Come to Know It?"* Swissotel, Boston, November 5–7.

Haggett, Louise, Tara Hanson and Megan Solo. 1997. "What Factors Contribute to Catholic Priests Breaking Their Vows of Celibacy/Chastity?" Unpublished.

Haywood, Thomas W., Howard M. Kravitz, Linda S. Grossman, Orest E. Wasylow, Daniel W. Hardy. 1996. "Psychological Aspects of Sexual Functioning Among Cleric and Non-Cleric Alleged Sex Offenders." *Child Abuse & Neglect.* 20:527–536.

Hensley, Christopher. 2001. "Exploring the Dynamics of Masturbation and Consensual Same Sex Activity within a Male Maximum Security Prison." *The Journal of Men's Studies.* 1:59–71.

———.1997. "From Behind the Walls of Confinement: an Analysis of Mississippi Prisoners' Attitude toward Sexuality." *Dissertation Abstracts International Section A: Humanities & Social Sciences.* 58:2857.

Hermand, Pierre. 1965. *The Priest: Celibate or Married.* Baltimore: Helicon. Original French title (1963): "Condition du Prête et marriage ou célibat?" Paris: Calmann-Levy.

Hill, C.T., Z. Rubin, and L.A. Peplau, L. A. 1976. "Breakups before marriage: The end of 102 affairs." In Jones, Warren: "Loneliness and Social Behavior" in *Loneliness. A Sourcebook of Current Theory, Research and Therapy*, edited by Lititia Anne Peplau and Daniel Perlman, NY: Wiley.

Hogan-Albach, Susan. 2004. USCCB committee bishops accused of abuse cover-up. 3 members of panel named in lawsuits; criticism called unfair. *Dallas Morning News,* January 19.

Hoge, Dean R. 2002. *The First Five Years of the Priesthood. A Study of Newly Ordained Catholic Priests.* Collegeville, MN: The Liturgical Press.

Humphreys, Laud. 1970, 1975. *Tearoom Trade. Impersonal sex in public places.* Hawthorne, NY: Aldine de Gruyter.

Ibrahim, Azmy Ishal. 1974. "Deviant Sexual Behavior in Men's Prisons." *Crime and Delinquency.* 20:38–44.

Jaffe, Richard M. 2001. *Neither Monk nor Layman: Clerical marriage in modern Japanese Buddhism.* NJ: Princeton University Press.

Jenkins, Philip. 1996. *Pedophiles and priests. Anatomy of a Contemporary Crisis.* NY: Oxford University Press.

Jones, Warren H. 1982. "Loneliness and Social Behavior." Ch. 15 in *Loneliness. A Sourcebook of Current Theory, Research and Therapy,* edited by Lititia Anne Peplau and Daniel Perlman. NY: Wiley.

Jones, W. H. and M.D. Carver. 1991. "Adjustment and coping implications of loneliness," in: Jari-Erik Nurmi, Sari Toivonen, Katariina Salmela-Aro, and Sana Eronen. 1997. "Social Strategies and Loneliness." *Journal of Social Psychology.* 137:764–778.

Jones, Warren H., R.O. Hansson, and T.G. Smith. 1980. "Loneliness and love: Implications for psychological and interpersonal functioning, in Loneliness and Social Behavior." *Loneliness. A Sourcebook of Current Theory, Research and Therapy,* edited by Lititia Anne Peplau and Daniel Perlman. NY: Wiley

Kalichman, Seth C. 1991. "Psychopathology and Personality Characteristics of Criminal Sexual Offenders as a Function of Victim Age." *Archives of Sexual Behavior.* 2:187–197.

Kendall-Tackett, K.A., L. M. Williams, and D. Finkelhor. 1993. "Impact of Sexual Abuse on Children: A Review and Synthesis of recent Empirical Studies." *Psychological Bulletin* 113:164–180.

Kennedy, Eugene. 1993. "Sex Abuse and Catholic Clerical Culture." *National Catholic Reporter,* March 19.

Kennedy, Eugene C., V.J. Heckler, F.J. Kobler and R.E. Walker. 1977. "Clinical assessment of a profession: Roman Catholic clergymen." *Journal of Clinical Psychology.* 33:120–128.

Kercher, Glen A. and Marilyn McShane. 1984. "The Prevalence of Child Sexual Abuse Victimization in an Adult Sample of Texas Residents." *Child Abuse & Neglect.* 8:495–501.

Kim, Oksoo. 1997. "Loneliness: A predictor of health perceptions among older Korean immigrants." *Psychological Reports.* 81:591–594.

Kornblum, Janet. 2005. For Steinem, these are the glory years. *USA Today,* February 2.

Long, Gary Thomas. 1993. "Homosexual Relationships in a Unique Setting: The Male Prison." *Homosexual Issues in the Workplace,* edited by Louis Diamant. 8:143–159.

Loos, Michael D. 2002. "The synergy of depravity and loneliness in alcoholism: A new conceptualization, and old problem." *Counseling & Values.* 46:199–212.

Lynch, Gerald W., Michele Galietta, Margaret Leland Smith, James Levine, Maureen O'Connor, Steven Penrod, Louis Schlesinger, Karen Terry. 2004 *The Nature and Scope of Sexual Abuse of Minors by Catholic Priests and Deacons in the United States 1950–2002.* NY: The John Jay College of Criminal Justice.

Magills Dictionary. 1998. Edited by D. Dawson. Westerville, OH: Hans & Cassidy.

Marsa, Fiona, Gary O'Reilly, Alan Carr, Paul Murphy, Maura O'Sullivan, Anthony Cotter, and Davi Hevey. 2004. "Attachment Styles and Psychological Profiles of Child Sex Offenders in Ireland." *Journal of Interpersonal Violence.* 19:228–251.

Marshall, Gordon. 1994, 1996. *The Concise Oxford Dictionary of Sociology.* NY: Oxford U. Press.

Marshall, W.L. 1989. "Intimacy, loneliness and sexual offenders," in Rokach, Ami. 2001. "Criminal offense type and the causes of 'loneliness'." *Journal of Psychology.* 135:277–291.

Maslow, Abraham H. 1987, 1954. *Motivation and Personality.* NY: Harper & Row.

McCaffrey, Joseph D., Monica Maske. 1993. "3 Men Sue South Jersey Priest for Sex Abuse." *The Star-Ledger,* June 11.

McCarthy, James F. 2002. Bishop Quinn exits abuse panel. *Cleveland Plain Dealer,* September 10.

McLaughlin, Barbara R. 1994. "Devastated Spirituality: The Impact of Clergy Sexual Abuse on the Survivor's Relationship with God and the Church." *Sexual Addiction & Compulsivity.*[1]

Medora, Nilufer P.; John C. Woodward. 1991. "Factors associates with loneliness among alcoholics in rehabilitation centers." *Journal of Social Psychology.* 131:769–779).

Money, John. 1980. *Love and Love Sickness.* Baltimore: Johns Hopkins University Press.

Moore, K., C. Nord, and J. Peterson. 1989. "Nonvoluntary Sexual Activity among Adolescents. *Family Planning Perspectives.* 21: 110–14.

Morris, Charles R. 1997. *American Catholic.* NY: Vintage.

Musolf, Gil Richard. 1992. "Structure, Institutions, Power & Ideology: New Directions within Symbolic Interactionism. *Sociological Quarterly,* 33:184.

Nacci, Peter L., Thomas R. Kane. 1984. Inmate Sexual Aggression: Some Evolving Propositions, Empirical Findings, and Mitigating Counter-forces. *Journal of Offender Counseling, Services & Rehabilitation. Special Issue: Gender issues, sex offenses, and criminal justice: Current trends.* 9:1–20.

————. 1983. "The Incidence of Sex and Sexual Aggression in Federal Prisons." *Federal Probation.* 47:31–36.

National Opinion Research Center (NORC). 1972. *The Catholic priest in the United States: Sociological investigations.* Andrew Greeley and Richard A. Schoenherr, principal investigators. Washington, D.C.: US Catholic Conference.

*New York Times.*1993. "Pope: Celibacy Is Not Essential to the Priesthood." July 18.

Nurmi, Jari-Erik, Sari Toivonen, Katariina Salmela-Aro, and Sana Eronen. 1997. "Social Strategies and Loneliness." *Journal of Social Psychology.* 137:764–778.

The Official Catholic Directory. 1996. Edited by Kenedy, P.J. & Sons. New Providence, NJ: Reed.

Ostling, Richard N. 1993. "Sex and the Single Priest." *Time,* July 5.

Ostling, Richard N. 1991. "Handmaid or Feminist?" *Time,* December 30.

Our Sunday Visitor's Catholic Encyclopedia. Huntington, IN: Our Sunday Visitor Pub.

Peplau, Lititia Anne, Daniel Perlman, eds. 1982. *Loneliness. A Sourcebook of Current Theory, Research and Therapy.* NY: Wiley

Peters, S.D., G.E. Wyatt, and D. Finkelhor. 1986. "Prevalence." Pp. 15–59 in *A Sourcebook on Child Sexual Abuse,* edited by D. Finkelhor. Beverly Hills, CA: Sage.

Powers, William T. 1973. *Behavior: The Control of Perception.* Chicago: Aldine.

Quinn, A. James. 1991. NCCB Guidelines and other considerations in pedophilia cases. Presented in 1990 in Columbus, Ohio, at the Midwest Canon Law Society.

Rice, David.1990. *Shattered Vows. Priests Who Leave.* NY: Triumph Books.

Rich, Vera. 1999. "Marry now . . . or not at all." *London Tablet,* October 23.

Richardson, John D. 2004. "Isolating frequency scale effects on self-reported loneliness." *Personality & Individual Differences.* 36: 235–244.

Rokach, Ami. 2001. "Criminal offense type and the causes of loneliness." *Journal of Psychology.* 135:277–291.

————. 2000a. "Offense type and the experience of 'loneliness'." *International Journal of Offender Therapy & Comparative Criminology.* 44:549–563.

————. 2000b. "Perceived Causes of Loneliness in Adulthood." *Journal of Social Behavior & Personality.* 15:67–85.

————. 1990. "Surviving and coping with 'loneliness'." *Journal of Psychology.* 124:39–54.

Rokach, Ami, Heather, Brock. 1997. Loneliness: A multidimensional experi-
    ence. *Psychology: A Journal of Human Behavior.* 34(1):1–9.

Rokach, Ami, Koledin, Spomenka. (1997). "Loneliness in jail: A study of the
    loneliness of incarcerated men." *International Journal of Offender Therapy &
    Comparative Criminology.* 4:168–179.

Rook, K.S. "Research on social support loneliness and social isolation: Toward an
    integration," in: Akerlind, Ingemar. 1992. "'Loneliness' and alcohol abuse: A
    review of evidences of an interplay." *Social Science & Medicine.* 34:405–414.

Rossetti, Stephen J. 1994. "Priest Suicides and the Crisis of Faith." *America
    Magazine,* October 29.

Rothenberg, Robert E. 1995. *The Plain Language Law Dictionary.* NY: Penguin.

Rubinstein, C. and Shaver, P. 1980. "Loneliness in two northeastern cities," in
    The Anatomy of Loneliness, edited by J. Hortag and J. Andy. NY: International
    Universities Press.

Russell, D. 1983. "The Incidence and Prevalence of Intrafamilial and Extra-
    familial Sexual Abuse of Female Children." *Child Abuse & Neglect.*
    7:133–146.

Russell, Daniel. 1982. "The Measurement of loneliness." Ch. 6, in *Loneliness.
    A Sourcebook of Current Theory, Research and Therapy,* edited by Peplau,
    Lititia Anne, Daniel Perlman. NY: Wiley

Russell, Daniel, L. A. Peplau, and C. Cutrona. 1980. "The revised UCLA Lone-
    liness Scale: Concurrent and discriminant validity evidence," in Jones,
    Warren H. (1982). Loneliness and Social Behavior. Ch. 15 in *Loneliness. A
    Sourcebook of Current Theory, Research and Therapy,* edited by. Lititia Anne
    Peplau and Daniel Perlman. NY: Wiley..

Schaeffer, Pamela. 1997. "Breaking Silence: Priests with AIDS Are Eager to
    Talk." *National Catholic Reporter,* April 18.

Schneider, Hans. 1997. "Sexual abuse of children: Strengths and weaknesses of
    current criminology." *International Journal of Offender Therapy & Com-
    parative Criminology.* 41:310–324.

Schoenherr, Richard A. and David Yamane. 2002. *Goodbye Father.* NY: Oxford.

Schoenherr, Richard and Lawrence Young. 1993. *Full Pews and Empty Altars.*
    Madison, WI: U. of Wis. Press.

———. 1990. "Quitting the Clergy: Resignations in the Roman Catholic
    Priesthood." *Journal for the Scientific Study of Religion.* 29:463–481.

Sedlak, A. 1991. *National Incidence and Prevalence of Child Abuse and Neglect:
    1988.* Revised Report. Rockville, MD: Westat.

Simmel, Georg. 1995, 1903. "The Web of Group Affiliations." *The Emergence of
    Sociological Theory,* edited by Serina Beauparlant. Belmont, CA: Wadsworth.

Simpson, J.A. and E. S. C. Weiner. 1989. *The Oxford Dictionary.* Oxford:
    Clarendon Press.

Sipe, A. W. Richard. 2003. *Celibacy in Crisis. A Secret World Revisited.* NY:

Brunner Routledge.

———. 1995. *Sex, Priests and Power. Anatomy of a Crisis.* NY: Brunner Mazel.

———. 1990. *A Secret World: Sexuality and the Search for Celibacy.* NY: Brunner Mazel.

Sullivan, Richard. 1970. "Comment—The Pros and Cons of Conjugal Visits in Prison Institutions." *Journal of Family Law.* 9:436–440.

Staff Reports. 2004. Bishops accused of sexual misconduct. CST, January 21. *(http://www.wfaa.com/s/dws/spe/2002/bishops/stories/ 061202dnmetbishside.1d915.html)* Retrieved March 14, 2004.

Stravinskas, Rev. Peter M. J. 1991. *Our Sunday Visitor's Catholic Encyclopedia.* Huntington, IN: Our Sunday Visitor Publishing.

Sutherland, Edwin H. 1992. "Sutherland's Theory: An Example of a Socialization Theory." *Sociology of Deviant Behavior,* edited by Marshall B. Clinard and Robert F. Meier. FL: Harcourt.

Thomas, Gordon. 1986. *Desire and Denial: celibacy and the church.* Boston: Little, Brown.

Thomas, Judy. 2000. "Report Explores AIDS, Priests." *Associated Press in Kansas City Star.* Kansas City, MO., January 29. *(http//www.kcstar.com/item/pages/home.pat,local/37743133.129.html).* Retrieved January 20, 2000.

Tomasello, Michael, Ann Cole Kruger, Hilary Horn Ratner. 1993. "Cultural Learning." *Behavioral and Brain Sciences,* 16:495–552.

Turner, Jonathan H. 1995. *Sociological Theory.* Belmont, CA: Wadsworth Publishing.

Van Wormer, Katherine, Frederick L. Bates. 1979. "A Study of Leadership Roles in an Alabama Prison for Women." *Human Relations.* 32:793–801.

Ward, David A. and Gene G. Kassebaum. 1964. "Homosexuality: A Mode of Adaptation in a Prison for Women." *Social Problems.* 159–177.

Merriam Webster's Dictionary of Law. 1996. Springfield, MA: Merriam Webster.

Webster's Seventh New Collegiate Dictionary. 1969. Springfield, MA: Merriam Webster.

Weiss, R.S. 1982. "Issues in the study of loneliness." Ch. 5 in *Loneliness. A Sourcebook of Current Theory, Research and Therapy,* edited by Lititia Anne Peplau and Daniel Perlman. NY: Wiley

———. 1973. "Loneliness: The experience of emotional and social isolation." In: Jones, Warren H. 1982. "Loneliness and Social Behavior." Ch. 15 in *Loneliness. A Sourcebook of Current Theory, Research and Therapy,* edited by Lititia Anne Peplau and Daniel Perlman. NY: Wiley.

West, Donald A., Robert Kellner and Maggi Moore-West. 1986. "The effects of 'loneliness': A review of the literature." *Comprehensive Psychiatry.* *27*:351–363.

Wilkes, Paul. 1991. "Profiles. The Education of an Archbishop II (Rembert Weakland)." *The New Yorker,* July 22.

Wimberley, Dale W. 1989. "Religion and Role Identity: A Structural Symbolic Interactionist's Conceptualization of Religiosity." *The Sociological Quarterly,* 30:130.

Winter Report, The. 1990. Archdiocese of St. John's. Newfoundland, Canada, 36.

Wood, V. Wylie, M.F. and Shaefor, B. 1969. An analysis of short self-report measures of life satisfaction: correlation with rater judgments. *Journal of Gerontology.* 2:465–469.

World Almanac. 2005. NY: World Almanac Books.

World Book Encyclopedia. 2005. Chicago: World Books, Inc.

Wyld, Henry Cecil & Partridge Eric H. 1969. *Complete and Unabridged the Little & Ives Webster Dictionary.* NY: J.J. Little & Ives Co.

Zonana, H., Gene Abel, John Bradford, Steven Hoge and Jeffrey Melzner. 1998. *APA Task Force Report on Sexually Dangerous Offenders.* Unpublished.